T0250207

Mad Eyed Misfits

Focus Animation
Series Editor: Giannalberto Bendazzi

The Focus Animation Series aims to provide unique, accessible content that may not otherwise be published. We allow researchers, academics, and professionals the ability to quickly publish high impact, current literature in the field of animation for a global audience. This series is a fine complement to the existing, robust animation titles available through CRC Press/Focal Press.

Series Editor Giannalberto Bendazzi, currently an independent scholar, is a former Visiting Professor of History of Animation at the Nanyang Technological University in Singapore and a former professor at the Università degli Studi di Milano. We welcome any submissions to help grow the wonderful content we are striving to provide to the animation community: giannalbertobendazzi@gmail.com.

Giannalberto Bendazzi; *Twice the First: Quirino Cristiani and the Animated Feature Film*

Maria Roberta Novielli; *Floating Worlds: A Short History of Japanese Animation*

Cinzia Bottini; *Redesigning Animation United Productions of America*

Rolf, Giesen; *Puppetry, Puppet Animation and the Digital Age*

Pamela Taylor; *Turner: Infinite Animation: The Life and Work of Adam Beckett*

Marco Bellano; Václav Trojan: *Music Composition in Czech Animated Films*

Mad Eyed Misfits

Writings on Indie Animation

Chris Robinson

CRC Press
Taylor & Francis Group
Boca Raton London

CRC Press is an imprint of the
Taylor & Francis Group, an **informa** business

First edition published 2022
by CRC Press
6000 Broken Sound Parkway NW, Suite 300, Boca Raton, FL 33487–2742

and by CRC Press
2 Park Square, Milton Park, Abingdon, Oxon, OX14 4RN

© 2022 Chris Robinson

CRC Press is an imprint of Taylor & Francis Group, LLC

ISBN: 978-1-032-20769-8 (hbk)
ISBN: 978-1-032-20771-1 (pbk)
ISBN: 978-1-003-26515-3 (ebk)

DOI: 10.1201/9781003265153

Typeset in Minion
by Apex CoVantage, LLC

For Jelena Popović
_____

Contents

About the Author

Chris Robinson is a Canadian writer and author. He is also the Artistic Director of the Ottawa International Animation Festival (OIAF) and is a well-known figure in the animated film world. He recently received the 2020 award for Outstanding Contribution to Animation Studies by the World Festival of Animation Film - Animafest Zagreb.

Robinson has been called "one of the stylistically most original and most provocative experts in the history of animation. He made a name for himself with a unique and eclectic magazine column *Animation Pimp*, which became a book of the same name (the column was later renamed *Cheer and Loathing in Animation*)" (*World Festival of Animated Film—Animafest Zagreb* Festival Council).

Mastering different methods and styles in critical and scholarly approaches, Robinson covers a broad range of Canadian and global subject matters in his books *Estonian Animation: Between Genius and Utter Illiteracy* (John Libbey Publishing, 2006), *Unsung Heroes of Animation* (John Libbey Publishing, 2005), *Canadian Animation: Looking for a Place to Happen* (John Libbey Publishing, 2008), *Ballad of a Thin Man: In Search of Ryan Larkin* (AWN Press/Course Technology, 2009), *Animators Unearthed* (Bloomsbury, 2010), and *Japanese Animation: Time out of Mind* (John Libbey Publishing, 2010).

In addition to his writing on animation, Robinson also wrote the Award-winning animated short *Lipsett Diaries* (2010), directed by Theodore Ushev.

Currently, Robinson is writing two books on animation and is working with German artist Andreas Hykade on *My Balls Are Killing Me*, a graphic novel about his experience with cancer. He is also collaborating with Theodore Ushev on a live-action feature film, *Drivin'*.

Introduction

HELLO. HERE ARE A few words to contextualize this dented tomb of gobbledygook. In 2006 or thereabouts, I put out a book called *Unsung Heroes of Animation* (John Libbey Publishing). In 2010, came *Animators Unearthed* (Continuum). Like this *Mad Eyed Misfits*, these books contained my scattered writings on assorted independent animation artists. The aim was twofold: I entered the animation world in 1991 with zero knowledge or experience. Given the scarcity of books about international animation I had to learn on the fly. So, I just dove into the murky waters and figured it out myself, viewing hours and hours of films and interviewing many generous international animators. Eventually, people started publishing my scribblings and once I compiled enough material it seemed logical to put together a book that would showcase and introduce these amazing artists to a wider audience. I'm not sure I succeeded, but hey, I tried.

It drives me nuts having to write this in 2021. Even though there is more animation being made than ever before, not a lot has changed. Then, like now, animation is little understood by the general public, or even most cinephiles. It's frequently associated with kiddie content or crass comedies for teens and young adults. In short, it's an art form that is rarely taken seriously by anyone. The public doesn't know about it; the cinema and art world look down upon it as facile fodder. It's a shame because these indie animation films are rich, poetic, personal, provocative. They are disturbing, mystifying, enlightening. These are the poets of animation. And while a lot of this work is accessible now thanks to Vimeo, YouTube and other streaming sites, these artists remain, like the toys in that old Rudolf special, stranded on Misfit Island, largely unknown outside of the animation festival scene.

Mad Eyed Misfits then is a sort of sequel to those previous books, this time collecting my assorted animated musings from 2011 onwards (or thereabouts). What is perhaps most encouraging is that there are many new artists featured in this book, a whole new generation of misfits who can't help but love this amazing art form. And it is amazing. What other art form combines music, painting, dance, film, video, sculpture, literature? Animation, someone somewhere said, is the summit of all arts.

Some acknowledgements before we begin. I want to thank Dan Sarto (Animation World Network) and Amid Amidi (Cartoon Brew) for allowing me to reprint assorted articles that I originally wrote for their online publications. Good animation champs, both. Second, a shout out to *Sight and Sound* magazine who, for a while, handed me a monthly animation column. Some of these pieces also originally appeared there. Finally, thank you to each and every animator included in this book. The generosity I've received during the last 30 years from these modest folks has been deeply appreciated.

Chris Robinson
Verdun, Quebec.
August 2021

CHAPTER 1

Masaaki Yuasa Speaks in Many Colours

A NYTIME YOU SEE THAT you're getting a new festival entry from Masaaki Yuasa, you feel a tinge of excitement, but when you scroll down the list and see two feature films submitted by the very same man, well, that's just orgasmic.

Already a cult figure in the animation scene, Yuasa added to that reputation in 2017 by releasing two stunning, contrasting and widely acclaimed animated features: *Lu Over the Wall*—about a displaced young boy who befriends—to the disenchantment of local villagers—a local mermaid; *Night is Short, Walk on Girl* is set during a seemingly endless evening of insane alcohol consumption in Kyoto. A young university student, Senpai (who some might recognize from the 2010 Yuasa-directed TV series, *Tatami Express*), decides to confess love for Otome. During the strange evening, littered with eccentric characters, Senpai decides to create some "chance" encounters to win over the woman.

Both films were immediate successes with *Lu Over the Wall* grabbing the Cristal for Best Feature Film at the 2017 Annecy International Animation Festival. *Night is Short, Walk on Girl*

DOI: 10.1201/9781003265153-1

then took home the Grand Prize for Animated Feature at the 2017 Ottawa International Animation Festival.

—

Like a fusion of Tex Avery, Dali and even—seriously—Danish philosopher, Soren Kierkegaard, Yuasa's work (which includes short films, TV series along with the cult favourite feature, *Mindgame*) bursts with visual energy, rapid fire colour patterns, sudden shifts in character design, elastic character movements. You're never sure where you are in this kaleidoscopic dance dreamscapes. Yuasa's work for film and TV, no matter the genre is consistently imaginative, magical and original. He seems to *get* animation. There are no rules in animation. You are not bound by laws of physics. Yet, so many animation artists can't seem to grasp that, perhaps fearful of the freedom. Yuasa shows no such fear as he gives us worlds and people that are stylized, exaggerated, distorted and impossible. Yet his works tell us more truths about individuals, relationships and society than so many of the mainstream animation frauds hell bent on regurgitating the same endless tropes and types no matter how tired, tedious and predictable. These counterfeits think they're telling us great stories about ourselves when really their breaths are as stale and staid as the corporate spaces that exhaled them.

Yuasa's work lets the audience breath. There are mysteries unexplained, left for us to ponder, to make sense of, or to walk away from. Every episode, say, of the extraordinary series, *Tatami Express*, is a standalone work of art that rivals any indie animation short. In it, he takes a fairly common theme of feckless post-secondary youth on campus and turns it into an utterly surreal, time shifting portrait of youth, identity, community and society. In fact, throughout all of Yuasa's work (whether it's the bizarre Romeo and Juliet meets flesh eating monsters series, *Kemonozume, 2006* or *Ping Pong, 2014*), we encounter anxious, feckless people sifting through life in search of a worthy purpose or at the very least a meaningful connection. It wouldn't be stretching it to say that the many characters who populate Yuasa's universe wouldn't be out of place in the philosophical books of Kierkegaard, who, in a different medium and manner, wrote in shifting tones, voices, names and styles (much like Yuasa's work makes frequent shifts in design and style) as he attempted to sort out the question of how does one live.

"I love both Tex Avery and Dali," admits Yuasa.

> I've been influenced by a lot of artists I get inspired with a lot of things I see, hear, smell, and touch in everyday life. I believe whole things inspiring me could be tuned into anime. Actually, the structure of tunes can be a model of storyboards when working on them. I often derive inspiration even from really modest visuals; a commercial, a cut from a movie, a movement from an anime as well as nameless flowers and grasses blooming on the road, clouds, stars, and moons in the sky. I'm also inspired with what I'm currently interested in and feeling. My humble wish for creating anime is to have common images, conversations, and scenes sublimed into art works.

In terms of his stylistic choices, mixed-techniques and wide palate of colours, Yuasa had to be careful

> not to get inclined to dark colours too much as both the movies are full of shaded and night scenes. I turned to high-contrasted colours while using neutral colours as well so that you sense freshness and vividness on the whole. I believe that things should be pleasant in principle and that is why shots get fresh and vivid in terms of colour design when characters have a sense of pleasure in the story.

Now, getting one animation feature out and about is an accomplishment in itself, but to release two outstanding—and refreshing—features takes some kind of special talent. Of course, Yuasa had no idea he'd be undertaking two features at once. "It was when I was making *Lu Over the Wall*," he says,

> that I got the green light to start the *Night is Short* project. I had to hurry and went into the pre-production phase while still making *Lu* because we hired freelance animators when we began with the production and we had to shift them to *Night is Short* before they would say goodbye to us.

While I wondered how difficult it must be to shuttle back and forth between two very different projects, Yuasa says that their differences actually made it easier. "They were quite different in visual style," he adds. "And that saved me from confusing their different movement styles of animation."

Although widely different in terms of tone, style and intended audience, both films are ultimately about love, kindness and acceptance—themes that we all need to be reminded of in this somewhat erratic time of intolerance. "*Lu Over the Wall* is a story about a mermaid who just wishes to make good friends with human beings," adds Yuasa.

> It's about overcoming an irrational sense of discrimination and prejudice, about understanding and accepting alien creatures. Similarly, *Night is Short* is a fable about how you'll only be happy when you wish for someone's happiness and you'll be unhappy when you just wish for your own happiness. Both movies depict how coming out of your shell could make things better. I love stories about opening up your heart.

Despite having only one moderately successful—*Mind Game* was a critical success but it was a box office failure. So much so that very few producers would even touch Yuasa after that—feature film experience Yuasa says that he rarely stresses out when he's creating. In fact, his biggest stress is finding support:

> I always enjoy making films but I must confess that I'd like to find more supporters and sympathizers and to make a commercial success. I really want to catch up with what people really want, but it is rather tough for me to try to achieve that.

Lu Over the Wall has all the potential to find a massive audience internationally. It's a gentle, soulful film that has many hallmarks of a successful family feature, but that is much more inventive in terms of animation, story, character and technique. Unfortunately, it's unlikely the film will make a big dent in the North American market. "Orthodox narratives attract more moviegoers," says Yuasa. "Innovative ones might not necessarily appeal to them. But I always dream of something that is both innovative and appealing to people."

Having worked in some many mediums, I wondered if Yuasa has a preference or if each offers different elements to an artist:

> I like to make features because you can see vividly how the audience sees your efforts, but I'm also enjoying making TV shows because they allow you to develop stories longer and in more detail. Also it is pretty enjoyable to make a short piece once in a while because you can make elaborately crafted ones.

More recently, Yuasa completed the series *Devilman Crybaby* (2018). "There's lots of sex and violence. I believe the story will make audiences cry, and is highly unsuitable for children because it is unexpectedly shocking."

I'd expect no less from this master of delicious and sorely needed unpredictability.

CHAPTER 2

52 Films, 1 Year

Meet John Morena

If you're going to try, go all the way.
otherwise, don't even start.
— Charles Bukowski, "Roll The Dice"

So . . . early in the OIAF 18 pre-selection process I'm skimming through the submission database and see an endless list of films (26 to be precise) by the same guy. Now, in my . . . let's see . . . it's 27 years since I started at the OIAF, that's a sure sign, as harsh as it sounds, of easy rejections. Anytime you get more than maybe 2–3 films from one person, you can often assume they're probably not so good.

Fortunately, curatorial decisions are not based on assumptions.

It turns out that there wasn't a dud among this gaggle of submissions that came courtesy of American animator, John Morena (who is self-taught and has worked in New York since 2000 doing an assortment of commissioned work including music videos, network promos, commercials and visual effects). Oh and it turns out that these 26 submissions were a mere pittance, as he actually made 52 films (yes, one for every week) in 2017.

DOI: 10.1201/9781003265153-2

What's even more impressive about Morena's parade of films is the diversity of tone, technique and subject matter of the films. Some films (e.g. *Untitled*, *Mini-Jazz*, *String of Sound* and the marvellous *Dreams I Don't Remember*) serve up abstract, impressionistic and stream of conscious imagery, while others touch upon prevalent social issues (e.g. *Dicks*, a hilarious fusion of an old educational film about the function of the penis replaced with images of guns, *Slurred*, a listing of the—sadly, seemingly endless slur words used against women, and *Flea Circus*, which attempts to put our oh-so-serious daily problems into a universal context).

The list of techniques is even more impressive as Morena makes use of flashlights, scanner, string, sound collage, cut out, ink, pencil, photocopies, polaroids, pixilation . . . just to name a few.

Intrigued and mystified, I sought Morena out and asked him what just what motivated this madness. "Fear. Frustration," replied Morena.

> I originally got into animation so I could make my own films. That was back in 2000. By mid-2016, I had a come-to-Jesus moment that I was getting old and had no films of my own under my belt. I had tried several times to make a film the traditional way but nothing ever truly got off the ground. I had a big time itch to make something.

Years earlier, Morena, who was getting fed up with the financially necessary but often mindless work of commercial animation, came up with the idea to do a weekly challenge that he called *Area 52*. "Originally," he says, "it was to be 52 experimental tests—one per week for a year—that I could use as a testing ground to discover new techniques that would then inform my regular client work."

Although Morena had no set rules in place when he began the experiments, because he was releasing them on Instagram he was forced to keep them under one minute. "It's one of the main reasons why I chose Instagram as the platform," adds Morena.

It made it so that I could actually get films done. A maximum of 60 seconds a week seemed more than doable if I was willing to sacrifice. Plus, platforms like Vimeo and YouTube are the filmmaking equivalent to the trading floor of the New York Stock Exchange. Everyone is crowded in the same place shouting for attention.

If there is a one commonality, aside from length, it's the minimal use of dialogue. "One of my self-imposed limitations," adds Morena, "was to make films that dissolve language boundaries. I used language and words sparingly, if at all."

Given the renegade spirit of *Area 52*, it's no surprise that Morena eschewed any exterior funding and paid for everything out of his own pocket. "I made sure to be really Resourceful," he says. "The most expensive film I made cost me $110. I don't see a need to spend thousands of dollars on a film that might just end up on Vimeo, be cool for a week, then fade into oblivion."

Incredibly, especially given Annecy's proclivity towards classical narrative films, the festival took 7 of Morena's submissions. He later learned that Anima Mundi (Brazil) took 10 and that the Hiroshima festival took a few (Ottawa has yet to announced their selection). "I was surprised that any festival wanted to include them," admits Morena. "I wouldn't consider my films 100% experimental but they definitely aren't standard fare and they also aren't for everyone. As for Annecy, I was stunned. Still am. I mean, Annecy is the crème de la crème."

With *Area 52* in the rearview mirror, Morena admits that while it was "the single greatest achievement of my life," he wouldn't want to undertake the challenge again. "Now that I've discovered that this is the way I want to make films, I can foresee another collection of films being made, similar to the way a band releases an album. But, no, probably not 52 of them."

Morena's approach reminds me a bit of another American animator, Steven Subotnick. From 1994–2004, Subotnick made four beautiful, highly crafted films. Then one day he decided to change things up, to stop being so fixated on making a good film. The results were astonishing. Since 2011, Subotnick had made 14 films, many of them festival award winners. I wondered if, given this somewhat similar—albeit compressed—experience, Morena feels that animators should spent less time on their work and maybe be a bit looser. "Less time on work is a subjective thing," he says.

But I do think that any filmmaker, especially young filmmakers, shouldn't end up like me. You don't want to stop dead in the middle of your career and wonder what would have happened if you had used to your time differently. I know that's still my burning fire. I'm 40 now. In 10 years I'll be 50. Ten years after that, will anyone care about what I have to say? There is literally zero excuse for filmmakers not to make films nowadays. It really makes all the sense in the world not to be so precious about it. It's a just a movie and 90% of the things filmmakers fuss over are things only they will notice.

CHAPTER 3

Passing on by Us

Clyde Peterson Talks Torrey Pines

WATCHING CLYDE PETERSON'S ANIMATED FEATURE, *Torrey Pines*, is like taking a long, satisfying and meandering stroll through the outskirts of a city. You have no idea where you are or where you're going. Instead, you're drenched in sea and landscapes enveloping you. You are *there* yet not. It's this calm, disconnected vibe that flows throughout this meditative cut-out animation film about a schizophrenic mother who kidnaps her preteen daughter (who is experiencing her own seismic shifts in emotional, mental and physical identity and takes her across the U.S. landscape.

It's strange to see all these beautiful landscapes in a hand-made cut-out film. Cut out animation is generally awkward, flat and, well, unrealistic in a sense. If you want to convey the power of landscapes, most people would rely on live action or photo-graphic images or detailed drawings. Not here. And yet it works because the truth is that in life, the landscapes we encounter can never truly be found again. They are all subjective experiences, touched by the emotions and context of the moment. Go back and revisit some special part of nature that you love. I bet it's not the same, cause, you're the not the same. Peterson's beautiful hand cut art—along with a hypnotic soundtrack that wouldn't be out of place in a Hal Hartley film—manages to capture—through the wide and innocent eyes of a child (and who is unaware that she'd been kidnapped). These continually shifting, drifting landscapes perfectly mirror both the mother's erratic state of mind and the girl's own inner transformations as she slowly starts to realize that maybe she's not only not into men, but not even into being a woman.

"I discovered animation watching MTV," says Peterson. "It was full of weird experimental animation. Then when Pee-Wee's Playhouse came on, I was hooked. Those dinosaurs that live in the cave in the Playhouse are my favorite." Peterson later studied documentary film produced and while working at post-production house in Seattle, got a chance to do some animation for commercials. "I was just helping out Britta Johnson, a fantastic Seattle animator. From there, I am self-taught."

The inspiration to make *Torrey Pines* was started following a screening of the documentary feature, *Persistence of Vision* (2012), which follows Richard Williams' attempts to finish the animated feature, *The Thief and the Cobbler*. "Afterwards," says Peterson,

> we were all just hanging out talking. Someone was like, "Do you guys ever make a feature?" Most people were like, "No." I was like, "I don't know. Sure." I can surely try and make a feature. There was like a change in my brain. Then I started thinking about what story I would want to tell. Clearly an autobiographical tale would be a good place to start.

Though Peterson had experimented with different animation techniques, cut-out animation made the most sense "because of space, time and cost, and because cut-out films look like a kid's movie and *Torrey Pines* is about a kid, so stylistically, it fit well."

The film took three years to make with Peterson using his bedroom as a studio. "I just turned my bedroom into a little production studio," says Peterson.

> I made a giant desk out of a door. I built a multiplane, homemade, animation stand out of one of those college student style Ikea wire frame dressers. Then I just took the wire baskets out and spray painted them black and cut a top for it with a hole for the camera lens.

Not surprisingly, the production team for *Torrey Pines* was about as minimal as you can get. "I had one employee who was also an animator," says Peterson.

> It was Chris Looney. He had just graduated from a computer animation school. He was really tired of it and ready to do some stop motion. We worked together probably for six months and we had gotten about 4 minutes of it done. It was good, but it was going very, very slow. We realized that we maybe could use a few interns.

From there, Peterson went on social media to look for interns. "Some," adds Peterson, "were good friends. Others we didn't really know at all. They worked one day a week for free and we were feeding them lunch. From there, things got exponentially faster. We just started the story board and then we split the story board up into scenes. We just tackled a scene a week. Some interns were really good at making foliage so we were like, 'Hey, you're on the cactuses.'"

The visual style of the film came from a love of American geography. "This will sound pretty cheesy," admits Peterson.

> But, I am totally in love with the nature of America and the vast, sprawling, empty spaces that exist in this weird, weird country. We have all these cities that are full of

people and then you just go outside of them and there's just nothing. You could sometimes drive all day and not see anything and I felt really captivated by that.

Water, in particular, plays a significant role in *Torrey Pines*, acting almost as a secondary character. "I wanted the ocean to be a third character," notes Peterson. "It felt really important to start the film and end the film with the ocean. It would be this grounding place."

The soundtrack, much like the ocean, also plays a pivotal supporting role in the film, subtly reflecting the power of the changing landscapes along with the complex inner states of the characters. To Peterson's credit, the music is not used—as it is in so many films—to pummel us into emotional submission. "I primarily make music videos for a living," says Peterson, "so I am often considering the balance between audio and visual impact on the viewer. How much can the music carry you? How far away will the image take you from the music?"

To help out, Peterson approached Chris Walla (formerly of indie band darlings Death Cab for Cutie) to work on the soundtrack. "He's an old friend," adds Peterson.

And I'm very familiar with his musical productions. He had never made a soundtrack before so he was excited to learn how to. And his solo record *Loops* is one of my favorite albums ever, so when we started to work with him, I hoped he would be willing to make his magical tape loops for the film, which he did!

Impatient with having to wait for festivals to decide whether to show the film or not, Peterson decided to do something unique by taking *Torrey Pines* on the road with a live band. "It's actually very rare for it to screen with the prerecorded score," notes Peterson.

My band *Your Heart Breaks* took it on tour right after its premiere in Seattle. I don't really believe in waiting for film festivals to give you permission to show your film, so we hit the road in a minivan for 9 weeks, playing 60 shows in North America with the live score. Then we did 2 European tours and were headed to Japan in January to screen it with a live band there as well. I have always felt that a film with a live score is the funnest way to experience cinema. We also have a live Foley crew from time to time. When we premiered the film, it was with a 14-person band and a 10-person choir. Total chaos, but totally amazing.

In recent years, animators have—unfortunately—been making louder films, relying less on imagery and more on dialogue to express story and emotions. *Torrey Pines*, thankfully, bucks that cloying trend, instead trusting in design, music and character to convey feelings. "I wanted to make a film that could travel around the world without having that many language barrier issues," says Peterson.

Less reading. Less subtitles and just visual story telling. I'd been studying American Sign Language out of interest in it. That was the core of it. How can you successfully do complete visual storytelling? When I'm watching an animated film and I'm just reading or listening and listening and listening to words the whole time I'm like, "Where's the animation?"

Ultimately, Peterson sought—and achieved—to create a film that serves as a sort of meeting point between "a child's imagination and adult hallucinations, to find that place where two people exist, are having dramatically different experiences but somehow co-existing."

Seems like an experience that could benefit the world right about now.

CHAPTER 4

Marcel, the King of Tervuren

A NIMATION SHORT FILMS ARE like poems or songs; at their best, they can house more riches inside a small space than many feature films or records. This was what attracted me to short animation films to begin with. It's not unusual to see, say, sprinkles of Buster Keaton, Samuel Beckett and Jean-Luc Godard spread generously through a five-minute short.

Marcel, The King Of Tervuren is just such a film.

Directed by American animator, Tom Schroeder (whose filmography includes the heart-breaking and hilarious, *Bike Race*), *Marcel, The King of Tervuren* is a Greek tragedy told—as only animation could—with Belgian roosters.

Marcel is a rooster who freely roams around the Belgium suburb of Tervuren waking up the neighbours each dawn with his distinctive cry of "CUCULURUCOO!" One day life takes a dramatic turn for Marcel. Suddenly everyone seems to want him dead. Marcel, though, refuses to go without a fight.

Based on a true story and narrated by Ann Merkmoes, the rooster's gravelly-voiced owner, *Marcel, The King of Tervuren* is an

DOI: 10.1201/9781003265153-4

existential tale of survival, perseverance, betrayal and mortality. Using a beautiful, energetic and freewheeling abstract paint style (notably during Marcel's fight scenes)—along with rotoscoped sequences—Schroeder precisely captures the chaos, uncertainty and violence of Marcel's daily existence.

Marcel might just be a rooster, but his struggle (although extreme) is one that most of us can recognize and empathize with. No, it's not everyday that our children are trying to murder us (well, at least not physically), eat us (yes, okay, one could argue that, say, social media is devouring us) or that someone is *explicitly* trying to poison us, but each day, each existence has its own struggles and obstacles.

What makes us marvel at Marcel is his defiance of death and seemingly pre-determined fate. With so many forces out to destroy him, you wouldn't blame Marcel for wiping his hands (well, if he had hands) and saying, "Fuck it, I'm done." But, he doesn't and that's something, that's everything. It's the classic Beckett line, "I can't go on, I'll go on." Who knows what drives Marcel? Who knows what drives any of us to go on? Maybe it's plain foolish stubbornness: "I'll go out, when I'm god damn ready." Maybe it's just for these moments when you can see and share in an experience like *Marcel, The King of Tervuren*, and leave the cinema buzzing, exhilarated, and just glad for the encounter, however momentary.

CHAPTER 5

"People Are Finally Listening"

Indigenous Animation Rises Up

THE WORLD OF independent animation has never been perfect, but it's always felt like a community that's *generally* been a step ahead of the rest of the artistic world. Operating, primarily, outside the animation industry, indie animation has long been a tolerant, inclusive community. That said, while there has been a pretty fair balance in Canadian animation in terms of gender, sexuality, region, there has been, until recently, a notable lack of consistent Indigenous voices.

Not surprisingly, the National Film Board of Canada (NFB) has been behind the creation of a number of Indigenous created and inspired works. Duke Redbird's 1969 short, *Charlie Squash Goes to Town*, was the first Indigenous animation produced at the NFB and possibly the first in Canada. In the 1970s and 1980s, a number of shorts told Inuit stories (e.g. *The Owl and The Lemming*, 1971; *The Owl Who Married a Goose*, 1973; *Summer Legend*, 1983).

DOI: 10.1201/9781003265153-5

Unfortunately, they were all (albeit with good intentions) directed by non-Indigenous artists.

In 2006, the NFB, in collaboration with the Aboriginal People's Television Network (APTN), co-produced the first two seasons of the pioneering stop motion series, *Wapos Bay*. Created by Dennis and Melanie Jackson, the series focused on life in a Cree community in Northern Saskatchewan. The show, which ran from 2006–2011, was aired in French, English, Cree and Inuk and had a positive influence on a number of Indigenous artists.

"It was so powerful to see our stories on screen for the first time," says Terril Calder, an influential Métis artist and stop motion animator based in Toronto. "I've great respect for the work that they put into the world and normalized it for us."

"Wapos Bay certainly did have a large influence on our early work and our company's evolution," says Neil Christopher, one of the co-founders of the Inuit owned, Nunavut-based studio, Taqqut Productions. "We started developing a stop motion series called *Beyond the Inuksuk* that never got picked up. This was our first big project and it was definitely inspired by *Wapos Bay*."

In 2009, again in collaboration with APTN, the NFB produced the series, *Vistas*, a collection of 13 films created by Indigenous artists (including Diane Obomsawin, of Abenaki descent, who has since become a well-known and award-winning animator on the animation festival circuit) from across Canada.

In 2019, the NFB's unique apprenticeship program, Hothouse (that gives emerging animators a chance to make a short film in 12 weeks), offered Indigenous creators from across the country an opportunity to create their own films. Chris Grant, a young Mi'kmaq artist from the Pabineau First Nation whose mother, Phyllis made two NFB animated shorts (*Maq and the Spirit of the Woods*, 2006; *Wasteg*, 2008) was one of those participants.

"It was an experience of growth for me," says Grant (who discovered animation at a young age through his mother).

> I was going through personal issues because I never lived in a cool city, had money and fun work. It was extremely

important for me as an artist because it boosted my credentials I guess for more work. It made me realize I am an animator and filmmaker at heart, and always have been. It was a beautiful fractal of growth for me.

Since about 2009 or 2010, Indigenous animation in Canada has also emerged outside the doors of the NFB, led by artists such as Terril Calder, Glenn Gear, Amanda Strong, Christopher Auchter and Taqqut Productions.

Taqqut Productions was founded in 2011 by Louise Flaherty and Neil Christopher. Their animation work, sometimes co-produced with the Montreal animation studio, e→d films, includes a mix of TV (*Ananna's Tent*) and short films (e.g. *Amaqqut Nunaat: The Country of Wolves*, 2011; *Little Folk of the Arctic*, 2015; *Giant Bear*, 2018, *What's My Superpower*, 2019) made primarily at younger audiences.

"The aim," says Flaherty, who started it in book publishing,

was to tell our stories using the language of the population of Nunavut. Taqqut's part is foremost to tell stories coming from Inuit with authentic Inuit content, using the Inuit language. Inuktitut is being lost at 1% a year, and if we have animated film targeting children to retain the language, there must be more made.

In recent years, the studio has branched out beyond traditional Inuit stories. "Our younger authors," adds Flaherty, "are now leading Taqqut with their vision to create film catering to all audiences. We have created other animations not just from oral stories, but also stories from our books. Not just with animation, but also with puppets."

In the realm of independent animation, Terril Calder has been an influential force since making her first stop motion films. Most of the work mentioned above has dealt with assorted myths/folk tales. Calder's work is raw, unstable and haunting, tackling a number of personal and difficult issues like identity (*Choke*, 2010, co-created with Michelle Latimer; *Canned Meat*, 2009; *Vessel*,

2013), memory, isolation and the unspeakable horrors of residential schools (*Snip*, 2016; *Keewaydah*, 2017).

A Drawing major graduate of the Fine Arts program at the University of Manitoba, Calder came to animation through Winnipeg's Video Pool Media Arts Centre. "Animation," says Calder,

> held and holds so many possibilities to tell my stories and bring a different perspective to screen to make change. It really is the sum of all of my parts. Activism, Storytelling, Art, Painting, Sewing, Photography, Compositing . . . it completely challenges me in every way.

After moving to Toronto, Calder learned 3D computer animation. "I thought becoming a CG animator would be a good career choice as a struggling performance artist." Calder found it difficult to find work in the animation industry. "Even though I was at the top of my class the industry at that time was pretty sexist. An older native woman didn't really fit into the hip work culture that they were trying to cultivate." In defiance Calder fused together performance art, storytelling and animation. Her experience with 3D animation convinced her that she need to work in a manner that was more intimate and physical. "I needed to get my hands dirty," Calder adds. My passion is exploring the physicality of the medium in Stop Motion. My first film went to Rotterdam and I learned so much very quickly about the power of the medium and all of the possibilities. Films get into the dialogue of people often becoming our frame of reference for knowledge and unlike the art I was doing I didn't have shipping issues . . . just a link to get it into the world. It's like it has a life of its own. It makes friends and it comes back to you. I was hooked."

After completing his MFA in sculpture/installation at Concordia, the Newfoundland born, Glenn Gear worked at a software development company in Montreal.

> I became increasingly curious and inspired by traditional animation techniques. I fell in love with cardboard cutout

and silhouette animation, but also looked at many other stop-motion animation processes with physical puppets. I began reading, researching, talking with other animators, and most importantly experimenting with as many techniques as I could with a small camera and basic setup. Although I didn't have a formal education in animation, my background in photography and sculpture greatly helped me. The ability to create a whole world, brought to life frame-by-frame, was addictive and pure magic. I was hooked.

Drawing on his Inuit and Newfoundland ancestry, Gear's films touch upon personal and collective histories (e.g. *Resettlement, Kablunât, Ikuma Siku*), mixed with more poetic and playful stories (*Rosewood Casket, Ginkgo, Cry of the Loup-garou*) all with nature (trees, animals, flowers, birds) often in a central role. Technically, Gear seems to throw everything into the mix: live action, cut out, drawn animation, silhouette, computer, archival materials.

"My early influences in animation weren't specifically Inuit or Indigenous," adds Gear.

I fell in love with the silhouette work of Lotte Reiniger, a contemporary of Walt Disney, largely forgotten by many. As a teen growing up in Corner Brook Newfoundland, I would take out NFB animation compilations on VHS from my local library, so those animations may have planted a seed in my young mind.

Christopher Auchter grew up on the islands of Haida Gwaii, an archipelago off the Northern Pacific coast of Canada. He studied media at Vancouver's Emily Carr University of Art and Design and later graduated from Sheridan College's computer animation program. Auchter has worked in book illustration, animated for various TV series and video games, and has directed live action (*Now is the Time*, 2020) and animation shorts (notably the beautiful and award-winning *The Mountain of SGaana* (2017), which told an old Haida fable).

> On the islands of Haida Gwaii, there are no theatres, still to this day," says Auchter, but in 1984, when I was 4 years old, we were visiting Vancouver, and I remember my Mom and Uncle Michael taking my brother and me to see our first film. We saw *Pinocchio*, and I think this had a substantial impact on me. My cultures, traditional Haida stories, were also a factor in me pursuing to learn animation.

Michif artist, Amanda Strong (whose animated shorts include the imaginative, haunting explorations of personal and collective ancestry, *Four Faces of the Moon*, 2016 and *Biidaaban*, 2017) came to stop motion animation through photo and illustration studies at Sheridan College.

> It gave me a basis to explore moving image while using these tools to create worlds and make stories move. Stop motion really is a series of photos that sequenced together create a magical experience of movement that can't be replicated by software. It is beautiful to see that first shot move after years of making all the pieces and it sure is beautiful when the sonic and visual pieces unite. It's a powerful tool to tell stories.

There are a variety of reasons for this recent rise in Indigenous created animation films, some of which overlap with the general rise in animation production. Advancements in technology have made animation a more accessible and affordable process for many. There was a time when animators were taking anywhere from 2–5–10 years to complete a short film. Today, there are a number of animators making films annually (sometimes more than one).

"Animation software," adds Strong, "has made animation more accessible to everyone. If you look just before 2009, that is when Flash and Toon Boom software was making a push into the lives of young artists."

"The tools and processes to create animation are more accessible and cost less," agrees Glenn Gear. "There have been great strides made in the past 10 years in terms of software, especially on alternative platforms such as smartphones. Apps like Stop Motion Studio, Animation Desk, and RoughAnimator are low cost and offer a streamlined workflow for animation. You don't necessarily need a large studio with specialized equipment."

Since the late 1990s, there has been a tsunami of animation programs and departments opening up across the world. To give the reader some context, I have been the Artistic Director of the Ottawa International Animation Festival (OIAF) since the early 1990s. When I first started with the OIAF in 1991, there were 750 films submitted to the then biannual festival. Today, the OIAF receives in the range of 2,400 films (including features, VR, TV, student etc.) annually.

The Simpsons (inspired by MTV and *Sesame Street* indirectly) showed producers and advertisers that animation could be profitable. This triggered an explosion in all avenues of animation and created a demand for talent. With the technological tools becoming more affordable, many educational institutions jumped on board to capitalize on the explosion—and to train and educate a new generation of animators.

Indigenous artists and youth have also benefitted—alongside increasing public awareness of the unjust and sometimes horrific manner that Indigenous people have been treated in Canada—from these advancements. "There is more investment into teaching Indigenous youth and providing them with the digital tools alongside traditional knowledge and ways of working," says Gear. "As more and more Indigenous folks migrate towards city centers, there are more informal and formal networks of knowledge, resource, and skill sharing. There is still much to be done in this regard, but the institutions such as universities, colleges and government institutions are slowly changing to hopefully be more accountable and transparent to Indigenous folks."

"We now have access to colonial tools and platforms," adds Strong (whose Vancouver based studio, Spotted Fawn Productions, creates space for Indigenous artists in animation). "It excites me to see more and more Indigenous people of all ages engaging with tools and technology to animate their stories. It's important that we lift each other up, celebrate our successes and always encourage other Indigenous storytellers to create."

"Our voices, cultures, and diverse stories are finally being heard by a larger public," adds Gear. "When I asked filmmaker Alanis Obomsawin l about the changes she has seen in the reception of Indigenous work in the past ten years, she said, 'People are finally listening.'"

CHAPTER 6

Fight! Fight! Fight!

Malcolm Sutherland's Bout

Gotta get into a fight Can't get out of it Gotta get into a fight Gonna blow you to a million pieces Blow you sky high, I don't care Splatter matter on the bloody ceiling Blow the building right into the air

—Mick Jagger/Keith Richards/Ron Wood, "Fight"

"I fight for perfection,"
"Do you achieve it?"
"Nah! No one does, but we aim for it,"

—Mike Tyson speaking with Charlie Rose

The bell rings. An anxious, impatient crowd gathers. The yin-yang ref calls out the opponents. One wears a bear mask, the other a snake. The bell rings again, pulsating with the calm of a Shinto bell. The opponents dance a slow, deliberate choreography of moves. Blood spurts forth into the raging, hungry eyes of the spectators, turning them into craving madmen. Blood energy soaks the minds and space. The fighters sever each other into oblivion before being reborn into a new unified beast with

DOI: 10.1201/9781003265153-6

the spectators. The lust for violence and death is complete. Spectacle and spectator become one magnificently frightening blood beast.

Malcolm Sutherland's short film, *Bout* (2011), explores wrestling, sport, and violence as ancient codified spiritual rituals. The film was inspired after Sutherland rediscovered wrestling and seeing matches in Montreal, Tokyo and Mexico City. "It blew my mind," says Sutherland.

> There was something intense and ancient about it that totally missed me as a kid. I was basically tripping out on the ritualism and theatricality of wrestling, and all those deep primal urges it satisfies. When human beings get together they seem totally insane,

says Sutherland. "Humans flock together around ideas and then the ideas manifest in the most bizarre and often violent patterns. It's like we lose individuality to something bigger."

I've been boxing semi-regularly for over a decade. Since I was a kid I'd always wanted to box. Already living a life drowning in anger, fear, anxiety, and sometimes violence, boxing seemed like the ideal solution—although I had no clue what the word "therapeutic" meant when I was 14. I did know that boxing could give me a space where I could legitimately beat the shit out of someone to the cheers and approval of others.

I never did sign up. They told me I needed to run regularly and get into shape first. That turned me off immediately. Running? Good conditioning? What the fuck does jogging or being in shape have to do with pounding faces into blood pulp?

In truth, I was relieved. I associated boxing with bad people. Only thugs, bullies and criminals boxed, so the idea of being around those people, let alone having them beat the blood out of me, terrified me.

Twenty years later I finally entered the ring. Married with children, I was mentally, physically and emotionally beaten.

I strutted in thinking that I was going to be an instant Micky Ward and start pounding the bags into dust. Didn't quite work that way. This wasn't a sweaty, dark room stinking of piss and filled with pug-nosed thugs; instead, there was an assortment of students, women and "nice" middle-class folks. There was also no ring or sparring. Instead there were different stations where you did skipping, shadow boxing, speed, reflex and heavy bag. The closest you come to sparring comes at the end when you smack the shit out of the heavy bag until you're completely drained.

"What the hell kind of boxing is this?" I wondered. "How can you fight without an opponent?"

Ah . . . but there was an opponent, there always had been: me.

Former heavyweight champ, Jack Johnson once said, "I made a lot of mistakes out of the ring, but I never made any in it." During my "fight" career I've battled addiction, abuse, depression, marriage, divorce, death, grief and cancer. As you get older you come to understand that the real fight is not in the ring, but in your life. That bell rings everyday. Filmmaker Hal Hartley summed it up succinctly in his short film, Ambition. The protagonist literally fights his way through the day from the moment he leaves his apartment.

Everyday life can pile drive us or send us to the floor with a devastating hook to the kidneys. I've had more knockdowns than some people have in a lifetime. That I keep getting up and staying in the round has a lot to do with what I learned through boxing. Boxing—or any other so-called "blood sport" exercises your mind not to shrink away from choosing what is difficult over what is easy.

Hard physical training can give birth to spiritual attributes like courage, patience, perseverance, selflessness, loyalty and compassion.

To achieve this state, you let go of yourself to a degree. In *Bout*, Sutherland speaks to a darker side of the transformative possibilities of sport, fight and spectacle, but losing yourself can also be an enlightening experience. It can be like a snake shedding its skin or a caterpillar re-born as a butterfly. We give up one for another. Identity is not something fixed. It's continually in flux. We dance, duck and punch through life seeding and stripping the muck of identities, behaviours and beliefs that outside influences (work, friends, family, social media) corner us with every hour.

Boxing (or running even—which I did eventually embrace) can help you shed the baggage of the moment as you move towards a state of calm, almost nothingness. When you reach that zone, you then start to rebuild and hopefully you emerge anew with your core identity in clear sight.

It takes mental and physical work to reach that state and it doesn't happen easily or often—even if you've been at it for 11 years. It happened to me recently, only a month ago.

One day everything seemed to click. Time slowed down. I forgot about technique. I forgot about my cancer results and coughing up blood that day. I forgot about my light-headedness, tingling feet, burning lungs. My feet hovered, my hands moved with no resistance. I couldn't see the bag or taste the sweat dripping on my lips, or hear the snap of the bag. I could simply sense the world around me, and it was perfect. It was heaven.

In *Bout*, the referee (drawn in the form of a yin-yang symbol) represents light and dark. The bout could could go one way or the other—or even exist between those two states. How we get there—wherever that is—is uncertain. All we know, as Sutherland acknowledges, is that where we go up and go down, there is something big existing beyond what we see or can control.

CHAPTER 7

Ghosts of a Different Dream

The Films of Mariusz Wilczynski

"**L**ET ME GO BACK TO the start again," sings a voice in Mariusz Wilczynski's hand drawn animated feature, *Kill it and Leave This Town*.

Imagine if you could have your family, loved ones, assorted heroes and idols all come together and reside snuggly within the comfort of your memories, no matter how fictionalized or misremembered (as Paul Auster once wrote, "memory is a story told a second time").

Kill it and Leave This Town does just that. Seeking safety after the death of his parents along with a close friend, an unnamed man (let's face it, we are in Wilczynski's memories) hides in the land of his memories where time pauses and everyone returns to life. Along the way, we meet an assortment of anonymous characters scattered about the Polish town of Łódź (where Wilczynski grew up). Eventually, the man realizes that even his subconscious river of misremembories can't stop time and aging and that he must swim back to the shores of reality.

DOI: 10.1201/9781003265153-7

Eschewing a traditional narrative, *Kill it and Leave This Town* takes the form of a free flowing dream, a collage of memories real, imagined and reconsidered. With its bluesy, soulful guitar driven soundtrack and assorted non-sequiturs, you feel like you're sitting in a smoking bar, slightly drunk, as the band plays through overlapping disconnected voices of the equally tipsy patrons. The result is a beautiful, messy, grotesque, heart wrenching and ultimately loving ode to a time and place no more, to people now gone.

—

Themes of nostalgia, loss and mortality run throughout Wilcynski's body of work. Prior to *Kill it*, he made a number of short films (*Times Have Passed, For My Mother and Me, Unfortunately, Kizi Mizi*, and music videos (*Allegro ma non tropp, Death to Five*), all of them carrying themes and elements that are later found in *Kill it and Leave This Town*. The past, in particular, appears to carry great weight in Wilcynski's films to the point where you wonder if it's a case of struggling to let go of the past or whether by diving into it, it better informs our next steps. "I think that childhood and youth are the time where we all experience our most vivid relationships in terms of emotions, like our most emotional friendships," says Wilcynski.

We discover everything for the very first time, everything has a different taste. The first cigarette, the first shot of vodka, the first adventures and events . . . everything is new. We feel it as strongly as possible because we're quite afraid of that and at the same time we enjoy it . . . . These are the primal, the strongest, archetypical first impressions. Maybe this is the reason why I come back to them so often in my films—these things have such a strong, honest, deep flavour.

Despite the predominance of a past gone by in his work, Wilcynski is adamant that while you can certainly learn from the past, you should never become a prisoner of your past.

You need to move forward and keep your mind open. I actually started drawing *Kill It and Leave This Town* to close the chapter on my past and get rid of it, to keep my mind open, and to come back to real life. I think I managed to do it. I settled the story with my parents, I finished my conversations with them, I finished my conversations with Tadeusz Nalepa (whose music is heard throughout the film), and thanks to that I don't suffer that much anymore. I don't have this kind of reminiscence where I would feel that I hadn't settled something with my mom, because I drew it in my film. My mom sees this, or at least I believe so. So I don't think that history teaches us something, but we sometimes need to take a look behind.

In a sense, we need to "take a look behind" so that we might let go and forget . . . a difficult task most days, but maybe especially during a rather chaotic period like the one we're all living in at the moment. Being present in reality is a challenge most days, but during this COVID pandemic, most are seeking any route that takes us away from the here and now. And as much as making *Kill It and Leave This Town* was a way of remembering to forget, Wilcynski admits that coming back to "real life" is a challenge:

Making this film, I did want to forget somehow and to come back to real life. I did not forget, but I sorted everything out, but the truth is that I dislike this "real world" so badly that I want to escape it by drawing another film. I am already working on it, and as soon as this activity, the festivals, and all the promotion-related arrangements around my current film settle down, I am "escaping" into my next film for some eight years again.

In fact, Wilcynzski's films, with their raw minimal backgrounds and design, along with the non-linear narratives all have a ghostly quality to them, as though they're a border or bridge between past and present, between conscious and subconscious. "I find it more of a magical element," says Wilcynski.

> This is why *Kill It and Leave This Town* takes place at a magical hour. We worked on this quite risky thing with Paweł Edelman, an extraordinary DOP, who worked with Roman Polanski and Andrzej Wajda. To Ewa Puszczyńska's (the producer) horror, we were making the picture increasingly darker, because I strived for the effect of the magical hour when what is real starts slipping into the unreal, and what is unreal starts to become real. That's an amazing moment and I consider it a very important quality for me.

Silent films, notably Chaplin, Murnau and von Stroheim, breathe throughout Wilczynski's oeuvre, but if you struggle to pinpoint his animation influences, you're not alone.

> I have to admit, honestly, without playing a hero, that it was my decision not to follow or look at what other animators are doing. When I was supposed to make illustrations for the TV programme about books, I drew 60 pictures, because I'm an ambitious person—it was about a minute and a half on the film, and when the pictures came alive, I got crazy and left behind every other art activity. The only thing I longed to do was draw and try to find my way to animation. And when I said I refused to watch anyone else or learn the technology, or read books, I really meant it. I even remember quite a funny situation. When I started my work at Łódź Film School, where I am a professor now, Piotr Dumała was (and still is) my colleague. He started talking about something and making references to some of his films. I told him: "Piotrek, I don't know, I'm sorry, but I haven't seen them." He was extremely surprised and said: "How come you've never watched my

films?!" The truth is that so far I have only seen some fragments of Piotr's films. There were a few films I saw and liked very much. It won't be very original, but I watched *Tango* by Zbyszek Rybczyński and to me, this is a masterpiece. It is also incredible for me that such an artistic film received an Oscar. Most of the Oscar-awarded films I saw are very safe and smoothened out, with a linear narrative. In general, I feel that I do not get influenced. I can also mention that, apart from *Tango*, I like Bruce Bickford's animation in Frank Zappa's *Baby Snakes*. He was a real crazy man. In *Baby Snakes* his animation resonates with Zappa's artistic genius in an incomparable way. On the other hand, I saw some other animations by Bigford and I felt quite bored.

Given the abstract or, let's say, "magical" elements of his films, it's surprising that there is not much improvisation involved in Wilcynski's creative process.

I do improvise during drawing. Sometimes a dot, a splat appears, I follow it in a way. The matter starts to become a narrative, that's true, but there must be some plan. If I were to compare this kind of work to something, it would be like a jazz concert. We know the main themes and we come back to them from time to time. We can improvise in between them, but we still stick to the somehow given direction. It's not like we can fly into the open space, say "To infinity and beyond," and go wherever the road takes us.

CHAPTER 8

Wondering Boy Poet

Bruce Bickford

I T'S HARD TO fathom that legendary American indie animator, Bruce Bickford has passed away. He was 72 in age only when he succumbed to a cardiac arrest on April 29th. Yet, in truth, Bickford never lost the essence of a child. He explored the world, seeing, feeling and discovering the beauty, terror and wonder of it all each day as though it were the first time.

Although Bickford achieved a cult following in the 1970s through his work for Frank Zappa, from the 1980s to his death, he worked in relative obscurity in his home in Seattle, continuing to create ingenious, baffling and mesmerizing line and clay animations.

Bickford's animations (including *Baby Snakes, Prometheus Garden, The Comic That Frenches the Mind, Cas'l, Atilla*) remain incomparable and indescribable. There was no one like him in animation. The closest comparison might be found the freewheeling jazz experimentation of Ornette Coleman or Albert Ayler or the freewheeling mystic streams of James Joyce. Nothing is stable in Bickford's universe. Heads, humans and landscapes form,

DOI: 10.1201/9781003265153-8   37

re-form, transform. It's like watching a child blissfully lost in play with his action figures. Most of the time you don't have a clue what the hell is going on, but you're mesmerized by the sheer inventiveness and wonder of it all.

And Bickford's world was never really meant to be understood, it was to be experienced, like life. As animation writer/historian Nobuaki Doi noted,

> Bruce's animation films are overwhelming. They tell so many things at the same time. He doesn't follow basic rules of animation (e.g. not animating too much). He makes everything move and the audience cannot keep track. It was only later when I met him that I realized that that's how he sees the world. While we see might see one or two things happening, Bruce sees everything!

"Bruce animates how dreams and even our darkest nightmares might feel," writes Nicholas Garaas, a stop motion animator who worked closely with Bickford as a manager/curator/archivist since 2015 and became one of his closest friends. "His works seamlessly bridged the gap between mesmerizing and horrifying while remaining mysteriously relevant."

During the last decade, there was a bit of a resurgence of interest in Bickford's work thanks to a bevy of festival appearances (e.g. Ottawa, Portland, Japan, Germany) and art shows. His work resonated with a number of contemporary animators. "Whilst I was studying at Newport University, I made a film called *Bluuuuurgh*." recalls British animator, Peter Millard.

"One of my teachers, James Manning, told me how it reminded him a lot of this animator called Bruce Bickford and that I should go straight to the University Library to rent out his dvds. I don't say this lightly but they changed my life. The passion, energy, confidence and uncompromised nature of his work was and still is a constant source of inspiration and assurance to my own work."

Bickford's influence extends beyond the animation world. Actor and director, Alex Winter, got to know Bickford while making a documentary about Frank Zappa:

> Bickford was a tireless creative force, and an inspiration not only to other animators, but to anyone who, like myself, was deeply impacted by his singular and hugely imaginative work. I feel privileged to have worked closely with Bruce over the last few years on the Frank Zappa doc, and grateful we'll be able to share unseen work of his, from past and present, in the movie.

Bickford was born in Seattle on February 11, 1947. One of four sons, Bickford was into arts from the start. One of the earliest cinema impressions he remembers was seeing Vittorio de Sica's *The Bicycle Thief*. "The part I remember," Bickford told me in 2015,

> was when this rich kid was eating a cheese sandwich. It looked like the cheese was stretching down. The way I remember it from my childhood was that it was stretching down so much that was it coming out of the upholstery of the chair. It was almost like animation.

The animation that had the greatest impact, surprisingly, given the complexity and seemingly non-linear layers of his own work, came from Walt Disney. "I saw Disney's Peter Pan in 1953," recalled Bickford.

> I knew about Peter Pan through a book so I was hyped up on seeing it but the movie itself exceeded any expectations I could have had. Whatever you say about Disney being cornball or anything like that, you've got to admit he was very tasteful. The colours in the movie are stunning. It was so exotic. Going to that island. Captain Hook, I thought, was fascinating. So many things about the

movie. I felt like I was transported to that land. At night for the next year before I went to sleep, I'd think about that movie and make my own version of it in my mind. I always hoped that when I went to sleep I'd dream about the movie.

It wasn't until he saw a Ray Harryhausen movie that he started to realize that animation was something he could do.

I could move model cars around and I was playing with plastic cowboys and jungle natives and animals and stuff. I'd sit and play with them for hours, so I had that habit. I was having a bit of a crisis. I'd spend hours thinking about movies and what I was going to do with my life. In 1964, I got an 8mm camera and that's when I started animating my model cars and making crude clay figures.

Bickford's artistic start was briefly put aside in the mid-1960s while he served three years in the U.S. marines—including a stint in Vietnam where he got shot at while defending a munitions dump: "I could see tracers in the distance coming out of the jungle splitting the early morning fog apart in waves as I heard the bullets whizz passed my ears."

The experience had a long-standing effect on Bickford's life and art. One of the common themes of Bickford's work is violence. His films are littered with bloodshed to the point where it's sort of common place. While Bickford never acknowledged the traumatic impact of his brief war experience, perhaps art was an unconscious form of therapy. In 2015, I asked him where he thought the violence came from: "I don't know. I guess I'm violent but I don't want to be in real life. It's too costly. We should all just take it all out through fictional means."

He returned to animating in 1969, exploring an assortment of techniques (line, cel, clay, stop motion). He began to get some attention with the short, *Tree,* and then he won his first festival award (at the 1971 Bellevue Arts Festival) with *Last Battle on Flat Earth*, a frenetic clay animation piece that featured the manic, hallucinatory epic violence that would dominate so much of his future work.

In 1973, impressed by the animation (directed by Charles Swenson who later worked for Klasky-Csupo on *Rugrats* and *Aaah! Real Monsters*) in a Frank Zappa movie, *200 Motels* (1971), Bickford headed to Los Angeles to meet the eccentric musician. "I went down to Los Angeles for work and I just went around town until I finally found the studio that did animation for Frank's movie. They put me in touch with Frank's main guy, Cal Schenkel. He arranged for me to meet Frank." Bickford impressed Zappa with some early animation. "It was like an extended bar room scene that went on for about 15 minutes and a battle scene and some line animation," recalled Bickford. "That initially got his interest and a year later they called me back. I eventually moved down and worked for Zappa for 6 ½ years."

During those years, Bickford was set up in a studio in Santa Monica and worked on two projects—*A Token of His Extreme* (1974) and *Snake Eyes* (1979)—both matching Zappa's music with Bickford's animation.

Working with Zappa was not easy (conversely, I'm sure working with Bickford was no picnic either). "We didn't get along so hot," admitted Bickford.

> It was the fault of both of us. He was not good at making movies. The projects should have at least had a production manager. And I wasn't cooperative when it came to doing what I was supposed to do. So it kinda went both ways.

In 1981, Bickford returned to Seattle and his mother's home.

> I went to work in her basement and she put up with me. It would be nice to get funding, but after my parents died, I inherited the house and enough of an inheritance that if I'm frugal I can last a few years probably.

From that time on, Bickford almost religiously worked on an assortment of projects ranging from short films (including the beautifully terrifying Claymation classic, *Prometheus Garden* in 1988), feature (*Cas'l*, 2015) graphic novels, unfinished scripts and begin to get a bit more attention on the art and festival circuit, largely stimulated by *Monster Road* (2004), a documentary about Bickford's fascinating and unconventional life and work.

To the end, Bickford never lost his childhood passion for creating or animation:

> Animation in my opinion is the great art form. Movies incorporate all the other art: design, acting, writing, everything. Animation is the most dynamic thing you do in movies because it can create things that wouldn't be photographable in real life. Things don't just happen, you have to make them happen. To me that's special.

CHAPTER 9

The Burden of Dreams

When the danger is so great that death becomes the hope, then despair is the hopelessness of not even being able to die."
—Kobe Bryant overheard during the 2000 NBA Finals

When you're chewing on life's gristle
Don't grumble, give a whistle
And this'll help things turn out for the best
Monty Python, "Always Look on the Bright Side of Life"

When I was in my teens, I worked briefly at a local McDonalds. Failing—and embarrassed to be seen—as a cashier I asked to work the overnight cleaning shifts. It meant working from about midnight to 7am, but it also guaranteed anonymity and solitude. During those shifts, there were many nights where the music was cranked and we'd (there was usually one other cleaner) turn the experience into a mini musical and sing and dance as we cleaned— poorly—the fryers, freezers and fridges. What else were we going to do? It was a shit job with shit hours and shit pay. Why not sing and dance through the night?

DOI: 10.1201/9781003265153-9

A similar feeling of hopelessness forms the core of Niki Lindroth von Bahr's animated short *The Burden*, a film that seems to fuse Gene Kelly and Finnish filmmaker Aki Kaurismaki into a proletariat/existential musical about an assortment of loners, losers and minimum wage earners working dead-end jobs in a dead-end world.

The Burden is divided into four sections: in a hotel, lonely fish sing about their woes, two custodial mice working late in a cafeteria perform a dance number, a team of telemarketing monkeys sing out the drivel they must repeat incessantly to customers, and, finally, in a supermarket an overnight stock clerk/dog sings as he observes items falling from the shelves as a sink hole appears in the supermarket floor.

Now *The Burden* isn't the first fish mini-opera (that honour, possibly, goes to an Estonian animation film, Mati Kutt's brilliant *Smoked Sprat Baked in the Sun*) nor is it the first working class musical number (see "Every Sperm is Sacred" from Monty Python's *The Meaning of Life*, or even the hilarious, absurd "Kool Thing" dance in Hal Hartley's *Simple Men* or Jean-Luc Godard's neorealistic musical, *A Woman is a Woman*), yet something has clearly resonated with contemporary audiences. The film has won close to 30 awards (including the Cristal at Annecy 2017) from not just animation festivals, but live action ones as well. It's rare that a single film singularly captures so many diverse juries and audiences.

"I guess that the feelings of boredom, pointless work and existential anxiety are quite universal," says Niki Lindroth von Bahr (who spent 2 ½ years working on the film), "I also like the idea of fishes in bathrobes as a world unification. Something like that." And certainly, in this time of repulsive inequality, the carpet bombing of information and a general sense of anxiety and terror at times, it really is no surprise that the film about an assortment of dancing worker animals has resonated so many people.

"For *The Burden*," says Lindroth von Bahr,

> I wanted to explore the outcome of colliding two very different atmospheres: the cheerful classical Hollywood musical feeling combined with the undermining boredom

of pointless work and existential anxiety in general. Our littleness in the universe framed in joyful tap dancing. I thought it might be interesting.

The film began, not surprisingly, with the music. "I worked together with the brilliant composer Hans Appelqvist, who wrote the music," says Lindroth von Bahr.

> He made the music in his own style, but according to my instructions about the atmosphere and the rough storylines of each episode (e.g. the hotel sequence would be low key and melancholic, the call centre was a cheerful Busby Berkeley tribute). We recorded everything live with a 15-person orchestra, (that killed our budget from day one). Then I spent a really, really long time building sets and puppets. And finally me and my colleagues animated the scenes in some tiny basement rooms in Stockholm and Trollhättan.

In terms of settings, you really can't find drearier environments than these ugly shopping areas that increasingly litter urban spaces. Plus, they're just the right spot to find bitter and miserable shitty wage earners. "I've been very fascinated," adds Lindroth von Bahr,

> by these kind of modern, generic shopping areas that you find along highways, perfectly designed for car driven consuming and nothing else. They remind me of lonely satellites, thrown out in the middle of nowhere. I think that I find them equally sad and interesting.

Animals have been the protagonists in Landroth von Bahr's previous films and she is very specific about her motivations for the types that she uses. "In *Bath House*," she explains,

> all the characters were inspired by recently extinct animal species. For *The Burden*, I used animals that are very

common in medical experiments such as the Beagle dog, the Rhesus Monkeys and actually a certain kind of fish called Banstickle. I did a whole lot of very depressing research, it's really not a subject that you want to image google.

Lindroth von Bahr (whose previous films *The Bathhouse* and *Tord and Tord* also skirted between realism and fantasy), took the most pleasure in building the sets and puppets. "it's the best part of the production," she admits.

I also find it interesting to find out how far you can take the level of realism in miniature models. They really mess with your head in an interesting way, like a sort of enhanced reality. Maybe we start noticing new things about ourselves and the world we live in. It's also just fun to create a surrounding that looks like your everyday life, and then add a fish in a bathrobe.

"Less enjoyable," she adds,

was shooting a 2-minute scene in Hotel Longstay with no pauses and making puppets tap dance was not easy for example. It wasn't an easy production and I had to work really hard for almost two years with no payment at all. Yet, I knew quite early that this film was going to be special and worth fighting for. So basically, I've been complaining a lot but I'm still very happy with the result.

Ah . . . don't grumble Niki, just whistle, dance, sing and feel all those ridiculous burdens fall, momentarily, from your shoulders into the vastness of the shrugging universe.

Feel better?

Good, me too.

Sorta.

CHAPTER 10

Unity by Tobias Stretch

W HEN YOU'VE BEEN WATCHING 2000 or so animation films a year for two decades it becomes increasingly rare to find a film that surprises you, gives you glorious goosebumps along your arms and triggers a series of profane verbal outbursts that bemuse and confuse your colleagues. Well, it happened this year courtesy of American animator Tobias Sharp's glorious music video for Christopher Bono's haunting choral piece, *Unity*.

Using the life and death of what we assume to be a transient man, Stretch seeks to answer Plato's question, "What is absolute unity?"

After a transient man appears to die outside an abandoned shack on a beautiful fall day, a trio of otherworldly figures appear (are they angels? ghosts? people from the man's past? parts of him?) and initiate a sort of ritualized dance of reclamation/regeneration with our hobo friend (Stretch calls the characters, who stand at over five feet tall, "puppetures." They are made of pvc, armature wire and various kinds of foam and paint.)

I'm not really much for notions of the afterlife (not that *Unity* is necessarily saying there is such a thing) or us having a soul, I'm

DOI: 10.1201/9781003265153-10

more in tune with the Heraclitus notion that we never step into the same river twice because we (including nature) are always in a state of transformation. I've always liked the idea that we are in a constant state of flux, that our physical/mental/emotional landscapes are always changing even if it's barely perceptible to others or ourselves. I like to think of the notion of "god" as finding yourself which harkens back to that ol' Greek aphorism, "know thyself." And maybe it's only in death—when we return to the beginning and merge with nature/universe that we can achieve that sense of harmony/oneness.

And that notion does seem to be at the root of *Unity* (although part of the film's richness stems from his mystery and ambiguity). It's only in death that this suffering transient finds a state of calm and balance with himself, nature and the universe.

Stretch's unusual techniques (a combination, he says, of "stop-motion, HRD, Street/Landscape animation and some frame blending in post") give the film (which took a year to make) a restless, ethereal quality. Nothing, no one is still. The landscapes, seasons, figures are in a constant state of flux and unrest in Stretch's time lapse/stop motion landscape. We're never sure what is real or unreal. Was the rural landscape merely in the mind of the dying transient man, perhaps a memory of a childhood home or was it the moment where his life changed before he become an urban street dweller?

Fittingly, it's the seamless unity of sound, concept, and visuals that elevate *Unity* from your standard age-old story about spiritual transformation/redemption into the sphere of the magical, ambiguous, inspiring and just plain soul shivering.

CHAPTER 11

Don Hertzfelt's Beautiful Days

A MERICAN ANIMATOR AND OSCAR nominee Don Hertzfeldt (*Billy's Balloon, Rejected, The Meaning of Life*) has been firing out an impressive body of work since the mid 1990s. Don't be deceived by his minimalist, stick-figure drawing style and comic tones: his work lays bare a rage of existence and madness that creeps and crawls within us. There are times when it howls to be unleashed upon the world, and times when it spurts out in a small shout, a dirty look or a middle finger. *It's Such a Beautiful Day*, Hertzfeldt's magnificent new feature film, does it all.

Watching *It's Such a Beautiful Day* is akin to reading the first chapter of William Faulkner's masterwork *The Sound and the Fury*. That chapter is infuriating, funny, disorientating and exhausting, and no wonder, it's told by a mentally ill character (Benjy Compson), or to take the full source of Faulkner's title, "A tale told by an idiot, full of sound and fury, signifying nothing."

With *It's Such a Beautiful Day*, we walk in the shoes of Bill, a disconnected, ailing man, as he drifts through the unreliable, disorientating fragments of his past and present. Bill sees the world

DOI: 10.1201/9781003265153-11

through small moving holes, and his many, fragmented social encounters reveal a man who is paranoid, obsessed, anxious and generally unable to connect with the world around him. It's only after overcoming a serious illness (we assume it's cancer) that Bill slowly begins to get it together and comes to see the beauty that life can offer when you're looking.

CR (Chris Robinson): **What are the roots of Bill's story?**

DH (Don Hertzfeldt): It began with a WWII story I read about Nazis invading a town. The protagonist is in a large group of people who are being marched through the city and across a bridge where they're going to be shot.

This man has lived in this town his entire life, but as he's being marched off to die, he notices details in the cobblestone streets he's never seen before. He sees new things in the faces of the people around him, people he's known for years. The air smells different. The currents in the river look strange and new. Suddenly he's seeing the world around him for the first time through these new lenses and it's disorienting and beautiful. It takes a horrible event sometimes to grab you by the shoulders and shake you, to wake you up.

CR: **Which is what happens to Bill, except that he faces a life-threatening illness.**

DH: Bill's been slapped in the face with something horrible and the world is looking very different to him: sad and beautiful. It's somebody facing death who hasn't really yet lived. The routine things he's used to doing are suddenly completely redundant.

You begin to see how death enriches life and gives everything its meaning. It's the people who drift around wasting their time, weirdly assuming they're going to live forever, that are the depressing ones, at least to me.

CR: **It's interesting how you use live action footage throughout. It seems to reinforce the disconnection between Bill and the surrounding world.**

DH: Yeah. I guess at its base it can be seen as a story about perception. The whole thing is seen from Bill's point of view and we're constantly hearing something resembling an inner monologue.

Having the animation run up against a sort of vague live action, experimenting with all the special effects, chopping up the story with fuzzy memories and unclear passages of time slipping in and out—these were all handy tools. There's lots of strange contrasts going on until it all sort of builds and combines in the third part.

We tend to gloss over so much of our lives. Memories go out of order. We take things for granted, rush around with blinders on and miss all the detail. We forget what's important and all the colour gets sucked out.

It's often not until something terrible happens to us that we're sort of shaken awake from the sleepwalking. Death reminds us we're alive. A terrible accident is on the news and for a brief moment a person snaps out of it and hugs his kids a little harder that night.

CR: **It's Such a Beautiful Day is comprised of three previously made short films: Everything Will Be Okay (2006), I Am So Proud of You (2008) and It's Such a Beautiful Day (2012). They were made as a trilogy so they fit together seamlessly, but I'm curious to know the motivations behind releasing the films together as a single feature.**

DH: I have to admit it wasn't well thought-out at all; it was mostly an afterthought. Once the final chapter was finished I toured the USA with the three of them. Afterwards I started putting together a new DVD of everything, and it seemed to make sense to offer them there for the first time as a seamless whole.

The newly minted feature film only subsequently played a small round of theatres with zero publicity until suddenly it was given an award from the LA film critics and was making all of these end-of-the-year top-ten lists. Then it became in demand at festivals.

Knowing what I do now, I obviously should have done a more traditional theatrical release for that version, held off with the DVD, positioned it better for all that awards season stuff, gotten a publicist etc., but all the great attention and stuff happened really unexpectedly. The DVD was pretty much already released, and we're still a pretty small operation here.

I'm still a bit disappointed in myself for underestimating the interest in the thing as a whole. But at least it's out there now for anyone to find.

CR: **How long did it take to make each short?**

DH: Each one about a year and a half, give or take. I took a few months off between parts two and three to go make a terrible cartoon [*Wisdom Teeth*, 2009—which is not a terrible film] about a baby being pulled out of a guy's face.

CR: **Did you alter the films at all for the feature?**

DH: I cut out the end credits of chapters 1 and 2 and added a new opening to the whole thing that I shot in my front yard.

And because I can do a lot of this stuff in HD from home now, all three chapters were given a much more solid colour correction than they'd ever had before. I spent weeks redoing almost all the levels in the first two and cleaned up a bunch of dirt and scratched frames everywhere. I also evened out the levels of the original soundtracks so everything matched up better.

Structurally, though, they're otherwise the same.

CR: **A few years back you told me you had no interest in making features. Have you changed your mind?**

DH: Ha, I don't remember that. I was probably deep in the trenches of production with nothing but the next two short films living in my head. Now that I've cleared them all out, the next project I'm preparing is in fact a new feature film. The script is pretty much finished and I hope we start soon.

CR: **With many indie animators now turning towards features, are we starting to see the slow death of short-form animation?**

DH: Nah, there's probably more people making animated shorts right now than any other period in history.

CHAPTER 12

Don Herzfeldt Talks
World of Tomorrow II

D ON HERTZFELDT'S MINIMALIST AND often absurdist stick figure work has been a fixture on the animation circuit since
his debut *Ah, L'Amour* in 1995. Although he was a success with
audiences almost from the start (to the point where he's been able
to self-fund his films) with popular and acclaimed films like *Billy's
Balloon, Rejected, Lily and Jim*—his work, for me at least, didn't
really start to get interesting until *The Meaning of Life* (2005).

With *The Meaning of Life*, Herztfeldt explored more impressive terrain. Poetic, playful and poignant, we encounter a world
of babbling humans, aliens and, finally, a father and son alien.
While these strange and familiar creatures come and go, the one
thing that remains constant is the beauty and mystery of stars and
suns of the universe. The meaning of life, suggests Herzfeldt, will
not be found in words, but simply in the mystifying and beguiling
nature around us. All we have to do is, well, shut up and look.

Herzfeldt followed up with an extraordinary trilogy (later edited
into the feature, *It's Such a Beautiful Day): Everything will Be OK
(2006), I am So Proud of You (2008), It's Such a Beautiful Day* (2011).

DOI: 10.1201/9781003265153-12

The protagonist of these films is Bill, a disconnected, ailing man who drifts through the unreliable, disorientating fragments of his past and present. Bill sees the world through small moving holes, and his many, fragmented social encounters reveal a man who is paranoid, obsessed, anxious and generally unable to connect with the world around him. It's only after overcoming a serious illness (we assume it's cancer) that Bill slowly begins to get it together and comes to see the beauty that life can offer when you're looking.

World of Tomorrow (2015), Herzfeldt's first full foray into science-fiction film (and digital animation), was a natural next step for an artist whose previous films dabbled in elements of the genre. Here, Herzfeldt continues his interest in identity this time via the mind of a young girl named Emily (with dialogue improvised by Hertzfeldt's niece) who meets her cloned self from the future. Through the meeting of the two selves, Herzfeldt explores, among other themes, issues of memory, mortality, identity, the charming chaos of childhood, and well, the sometimes terrifying prospects of humanity.

Given the success of *World of Tomorrow* (including an Oscar nomination and several Festival awards), it's maybe no surprise that Herzfeldt has returned to the same world for the follow-up film, *World of Tomorrow II: The Burden of Other People's Thoughts* (2017). This time, young Emily helps a fractured back-up clone from the future repair her mind.

As the new film begins its touring life, Herzfeldt very generously set aside some time to offer insight into his latest film and where he sees it going.

CR (Chris Robinson): **What was the starting point of the original *World of Tomorrow*? I know that you were maybe doing this to teach yourself digital, but how did you stumble upon this storyline. There's an improvised feel to it. Did your niece's "ramblings" help guide you towards a direction?**

DH (Don Hertzfeldt): I'd always wanted to write a science fiction story and "going digital" for the first time after twenty or so years was a great excuse to do it. The story I had in mind required a little kid and I didn't want to fake it. You usually hear adults doing child voices in cartoons and it can be funny but it never feels real. It's not the experience of having a conversation with a four-year-old, where every other thought is sort of out of left field. And getting that sense of spontaneity in animation, which is by nature the least spontaneous way to make a movie, is a really powerful thing. So while everything Winona said was unscripted (at that age her thoughts and reactions to things were still short and tidy enough to edit around and find a way to fit into my story), I rewrote Julia's lines so her half of the conversations made sense, but for the most part I was able to keep that movie on the path I'd intended.

CR: **Was the plan always to make a second film? And do you foresee this becoming another trilogy that can than potentially be transferred into feature that might reach other markets that short films don't always reach?**

DH: I don't often plan projects very far out in advance because one of them can take so long to finish that I sometimes feel like a different person by the time I reach the end. But about a month before *World of Tomorrow* was released, in late 2014, I saw my niece again and I recorded her some more, then at age five. And when I signed Julia up for the first film I signed her up for another one at the same time. So I didn't have a story planned yet for a second one but even in those early stages I did have a feeling I might want to go back for more. It was just a good feeling making the first one, the most fun I'd had animating, maybe ever. I also knew that, like the first one, if the new round of recording with my niece yielded nothing interesting, there would be no new film to speak of anyway. I figured I'd at least see if anything interesting would come from those new sessions, but I've never thought of this story as a trilogy.

The *It's Such a Beautiful Day* story is a very complete three chapters and very clearly a closed thing. What makes *World of Tomorrow* interesting to me is how open and free it all is. It makes much more sense, at least right now, as a five or seven or ten-episode thing rather than a trilogy or a closed feature-length. I think running times are thankfully becoming more and more irrelevant these days. Streaming has opened everything up, at least in the living room, and suddenly people are eager to binge-watch an entire series or just watch a great short . . . that 8-hour OJ Simpson documentary, I can't imagine that at any other length. *World of Tomorrow* was the first short film on Netflix and I was really heartened to find people recommending it to their friends and not even mentioning (or *warning them*), that it was a short. when I was in film school, we were warned to never, ever make a movie with a weird running time—45 minutes was considered absolutely suicidal and unsellable in all markets—which was true back then, but I think we're at a point now where audience's viewing habits have been allowed to evolve—and at the end of the day we just want to see something good. The playing field between short and long and indie and studio seems to be just a little more level. So, I've been kind of thinking of *World of Tomorrow* in those terms. It's a different kind of narrative, right now I don't see it becoming a tidy feature-length thing. The first two chapters mirror each other nicely but I think going forward we're going to break away from that and really see what else is out there.

CR: **In terms of both films, I also wonder how much of the vision changed from conception to final product. Was there a lot of freewheeling along the way or did you have a fairly firm vision of where you wanted the films to go?**

DH: The second episode is really where my plans went off the rails. I had a vague idea of the sort of thing I wanted to write about but the audio Winona delivered (at age five, plus a few recordings from age six) went in absolutely every other direction (e.g. long monologues about triangle land, caves, bracelets, imaginary friends, all sorts of wonderful very strange stuff that had just nothing at all to do with my original ideas). There was no clear way to make any of it fit together and it turned into an extremely complicated puzzle, just trying to make sense of it all. She lives in Scotland and I only see her about once a year, so it's not like I could easily revisit her for more material. These audio sessions are really take it or leave it, make a movie from these sessions or make nothing. So it was a very strange and uniquely difficult writing process, combing through all the audio and figuring out what she could be talking about *here*, and what on earth her character might mean when she says *this*. When it all finally came together and I was able to wrap some sort narrative around it all, it turned into something sort of weird and beautiful. It's like writing while half-unconscious or something. I was not expecting that to happen and I'm still sort of surprised it exists.

CR: **From the start you've always done things on your own terms. So much has changed since you came into animation and I wonder how the experience has changed for you. Has it become easier or harder for you to stick to your guns and follow your own path? How?**

DH: The technology has all changed from top to bottom but I think the basic philosophy, at least for me, has been pretty much the same. When I was starting out, the big goal was to maybe get your animated short picked up by MTV or licensed by an animation festival like *Spike and Mike* or something. If you couldn't figure out how to monetize your work one way or another, you couldn't make another film. There were not very many Americans in this field to follow, so when I was a student

I just tried to copy what the big studios did with their features. First, do film festivals and theatrical stuff, then trickle down to TV deals and then figure out something for DVD or VHS. aside from the thing I did for *The Simpsons*, I've never done any commissioned work in the twenty-odd years I've been doing this, so the short films always had to be profitable on their own. No way around it. To even make an animated short back then you'd need access to a giant rostrum camera—I eventually just bought my own—and all the 35mm film stock plus post-production was very expensive. There's many more ways to animate something today, and many more places to get your stuff seen, but the need for the films to be self-sustaining is the same. Instead of selling something to MTV now, there's the Netflixes of the world, blurays, etc. All the screens have changed but the idea's the same. I don't want to animate advertisements and I've never been given a grant. So the only way to follow my own path has always been to not rely on other people.

CR: **Did you feel more confident this time around with the digital tools? Did that make it easier to get through the production this time or did you stumble onto some new challenges?**

DH: I made the first *World of Tomorrow* on old versions of Photoshop and final cut, old at the time, maybe ten years old by now. When I was first figuring out animation on the tablet, I tested out a couple of animation-centric programs and I couldn't stand any of them. The brush options were surprisingly terrible. Photoshop easily had the best brushes and I was already fluent in it so I just landed there. Photoshop was very clunky when it came to actually watching your animation though, so I settled on drawing everything in there and exporting it all to final cut in frame sequences where I'd assemble and preview it all. That did the job, but both programs crashed a lot the more I pushed them, so fast forward to a couple years later, starting work on "episode two." I realized I really didn't want the look of it to change drastically from the first one, so I was afraid of upgrading either program or changing this little pipeline, because once you get a new version of something or leap into an entirely different thing like after-effects, all your filters tend to change and I was wary of the second episode suddenly having a totally different feel. So production on "episode two" was mainly more difficult because that movie expanded so much visually that this old software almost never kept up. Crash after crash. Made it to the finish line with smoke pouring from the computer. but moving forward now I'm feeling less tethered to having to do that—though I have to admit I still haven't upgraded.

CR: **While some would say *The Burden of Other People's Thoughts* is sci-fi, I see something more realistic and philosophical. In the sense that the film deals with identity, and specifically how identity is not a firm or necessarily reliable "thing" . . . it's constantly in flux, always growing, shifting, or even devolving. All these versions of Emily can easily fit any of us. e.g. I am, yet am not, the 5-year-old me, the 16-year-old me . . . the 34-year-old . . . and one day I won't be this 50-year-old me either. Granted, identity seems a lot more messed up (or liberated, depending on your perspective) in this internet age when we can take on any manner of guise. So . . . I'm wondering if that sense of identity as fluid was on your mind at the start.**

DH: It was, and I think that's also what makes our memories, also constantly changing and growing, such powerful things. If I said, "Hey, Chris, there's this new technology that will allow you to live an extra hundred years," that's a pretty cool thing. But then if I said, "the catch is, we'd have to reboot your brain and erase everything first," suddenly that's a lot less attractive. When you say you want to live forever, what you really mean is you want to maintain that fluid continuity of memory and experience. It's everything, it's what makes us who we are. To erase that feels like murder.

CHAPTER 13

Joy Street

Remembering Suzan Pitt

A FTER ALREADY ENDURING THE LOSSES OF Dutch animator, Rosto, and clay animation wizard, Bruce Bickford, the animation world lost another indie legend in 2019 when Suzan Pitt succumbed to cancer on June 16 at age 75.

As an instructor at Cal Arts and the creator of beautiful, personal, provocative short films (notably, *Asparagus, Joy Street* and *El Doctor*), Pitt's impact and influence reached far and wide within the animation world.

These days, it's no big deal to see women animators addressing topics of sexuality (no shortage of films about vaginas and tampons in recent years), identity, mental illness, addiction etc. . . . but decades before, this was not always so common in an animation community dominated (granted to a lesser degree than the industry) by men. American animator and artist Suzan Pitt was one of the few (that includes men too) who was making films that tackled depression, mortality, identity and sexuality in honest, hopeful and insightful ways.

DOI: 10.1201/9781003265153-13

"Suzan peered deep into life, into corners few dare to approach," writes New York-based animator and artist, Lisa Crafts.

> She was a radiant being—an artist, visionary, naturalist, and dear friend. She approached her work with a fierce dedication, a boldness, a sense of awe, humor and raw vulnerability. Her films stun, mystify and awaken. They are journeys, and a traveler can go deeper with every viewing.

"We first met," continues Crafts, "when she taught at Harvard in the 70s, and she became part of our small animation community in Cambridge. She was a decade older, and possibly the first fully realized artist I knew. She modeled dedication, risk and an untamed sense of wonder. She directed the performance, *Loops*, an evening of animation, spoken word and live music in collaboration with John Cage at Harvard. There was a sense of mythology swirling around her, yet she was down to earth, with a great sense of love and play. She moved fluidly between mediums, embracing interdisciplinarity before it was a word."

"Suzan was an outlier," animator George Griffin tells Cartoon Brew.

> florid figures and dream environments caressed by her brush and pencil, and just as surely an indweller, revealing her emotional life as few animators have. Like Maria Lassnig, another painter who performed herself, yet without using the "real" face to reveal the hidden soul.

Suzan Pitt's love of animation began in her childhood in her parent's house in Kansas City, Missouri: "There was a dollhouse in the dark attic where I would go to play," Pitt once revealed, "I projected myself into plastic figures, chairs, lamps and various objects. It was an escape to a richer world of play and imagination."

After studying painting and printmaking, Pitt remained unsatisfied creatively. She thought of her Kansas dollhouse and the vivid worlds and characters she had created in it as a child. How could she capture that world in her art? One day it occurred to her that her painted images looked like they were in arrested movement. "I thought of doing animation but didn't know anything about it." Pitt got a hold of an 8mm Bolex camera.

> With the Bolex mounted on a tripod taped to the floor, I animated cut-outs, paper paintings of living stuff (twigs and sprouts and unknown vegetables) moving through real grass I had made a bed for on the floor- that was it- an event.

During the early 1970s, while teaching in Minneapolis, Pitt made a number of short animations. The first significant film is *Crocus* (1971), a cut-out film that anticipates many of the themes (sexuality, creativity, relationships) of Pitt's later works. Another early highlight is *Jefferson Circus Songs* (1973), a bizarre pixilation/cut-out film made with kids and set in a circus.

It was with *Aspargus* (1979) that Pitt really made her mark on the animation and film circuit. This bold, luscious and overwhelming work is a giant step from her earlier films. Taking some of the visual aspects of *Crocus*, *Asparagus* is a journey through the creative process of a female artist. Like a work of free jazz, Pitt's imagery is open to multiple interpretations. The downside of the film's freewheeling nature is that over the years, *Asparagus* has sometimes been deemed a soft-porn film because of the sexual images in the film. "I thought of the asparagus as a beautiful symbol of sexuality," Pitt once said. "I wanted to make a visual poem about the creative process and take the viewer through the mind of an artist/magician as she searches for the forces that stimulate her creative existence."

Asparagus was extremely well received for a short animation film. The film premiered at the Whitney Museum in its own miniature theatre. Then the film was shown before David Lynch's *Eraserhead* and ran for two years in New York and then a year in Los Angeles.

In the 1980s, overworked (she was teaching at Harvard and doing animation for operas), Pitt suffered a breakdown.

> I think of it as some monster inside who devours myself and pulls me down under. I constantly have had to find ways to survive and climb back out, sometimes letting it sink me for long periods and sometimes fighting by brute force through determined work.

After months of therapy, Pitt channelled her darkness into the film *Joy Street (1995)*. Made over a period of four years, this breathtakingly beautiful painted film captures the extremes of depression as a lonely, suicidal woman finds hope through, of all things, a cartoon mouse that comes to life.

A restless soul her whole life, Pitt was on the move again in 1998, this time to teach at Cal Arts in the experimental animation program. "I get tired of being in one place and I like to experience different people and places, often taking my movies-in-progress with me. I need to be charged and awakened or else I fall."

After working on a series of paintings that she never showed, Pitt began work on, *El Doctor (2006)*. Using a script written by her son, Blue Kraning, Pitt uses elements of magic realism and Mexican culture, along with vivid oil colours to create a dazzling, haunting and poignant evocation of a man's final moments.

The film's protagonist is a cranky, cynical old doctor who sees the world as empty and ugly. Only in his last living moments does he realize that he was the one making the world miserable and that with a different perspective, the world was actually filled with possibility and beauty.

El Doctor was not Pitt's final film (She would make two more animation shorts: *Visitation* in 2011 and *Pinball* in 2013), but the message of the film seems like a fitting epitaph to an amazing and bold artist who frequently overcame her own demons and darkness to fill with the world with imagination, honesty, beauty and love.

"A couple of weeks ago, we were texting," recalls Lisa Crafts. "She was not well and the texts became quite surreal, yet always poetic and poignant. The last communication from her said, 'Enter the room with a sly smile.' I believe she did."

CHAPTER 14

Nightlights in the Forest

Cartoon Saloon

A GUY NAMED GABRIEL GARCIA MARQUEZ allegedly (I wasn't there) described his grandmother's storytelling style as telling "the wildest things with a completely natural tone of voice." The old lady is said to have told the young Marquez all manner of supernatural and fantastic stories, tales and gossip with a deadpan expression, as though they were the most normal things.

Something about that Marquez line overlapped with my experience of watching three striking animation features (*The Secret of Kells*, *Song of the Sea*, *The Breadwinner*) created by Irish studio, Cartoon Saloon.

In all three films (to a lesser degree in *The Breadwinner*), the boundaries between fantasy and an often harsh reality, are barely discernible as the child protagonists (each of whom has suffered the loss of a family member) embark on bold quests in an attempt to comprehend, grow and find light in a dark, cruel, yet equally magical and hopeful, world.

DOI: 10.1201/9781003265153-14

Founded in 1999 by the trio of Paul Young, Tomm Moore and Nora Twomey, Cartoon Saloon has created an assortment of short films, commercials and TV works, but their most impressive work, in my humble view, has been in feature animation, where they've created a trio of innovative and beautifully made films that fuse realism, fantasy, history and myth with striking handmade imagery.

While most studios shy away from risk-taking in animation features—sticking instead to familiar classical linear narrative tropes armed with cliché and tired character types that too often fail to trust the comprehension levels of their young audiences— Cartoon Saloon seems to thrive on being aesthetically and conceptually edgier while having faith that their audiences will grasp the layers of their work.

In short, they don't treat viewers like twits.

Cartoon Saloon's stories (incorporating folk legends and art, stories and myths) are honest and heavy. Accompanied by often dizzyingly delicious, almost abstract backgrounds—that give their films that extra dose of magic—the studio's work explores the pain, mystery and brutality of life as experienced through children who have been dealt some pretty harsh blows in life.

At the core of Cartoon Saloon's work is the importance sharing stories. The young protagonists learn from various adults (yes, adults are actually treated with respect and not dismissed and mocked as they are in so many contemporary movies and TV shows these days) that guidance and wisdom can be found in memories, tales and past experiences. Echoing William Faulkner's famous line, "the past is never dead, it's not even past," the children learn that while the past is not fixed, it can serve as a guide to the present for the future.

In the end, no one goes it alone. Enlightenment is a collaborative effort between child and adult. Yet, ultimately, it is the beautifully stubborn, naïve and determined passion of the children—ignorant of the crippling doubt, anxiety and resignation that haunts the adults (e.g. the Uncle in *Secret of Kells*, the father in *Song of the Sea*, the family in *The Breadwinner*)—that saves the day and finds the light, however dim, in the surrounding darkness.

CHAPTER 15

Beautiful Maladies

The Uncanny World of Rosto

THE AWARD-WINNING DUTCH ANIMATOR, Rosto—who passed away from lung cancer on March 7, 2019—was a polarizing figure in the animation world ("I'm a niche within a niche within a niche," he once said of his place in the animation village). His dark (some might say, Goth) hybrid, mixed media films (e.g *Jona/Tomberry, Lonely Bones, Splintertime, Reruns*) zippered together live action, digital animation, and traditional animation into an uncomfortable and indefinable beast that riled some and amazed more.

His biggest success came in animation, yet he never considered himself an animator—which also ruffled the sensitive feathers of some animators: "I don't say this because I'm a snob," he told me in 2015, "I say this because an animator is a profession and people are really good at it and few qualify at it, which is animating stuff. Although I do it, I do tons of other things."

Whatever your opinion, Rosto's work remains unlike anything else out there in the film landscape. Born of dreams, nightmares, memories and a whole whack of subconscious imagery

DOI: 10.1201/9781003265153-15

and thoughts, Rosto's work swam frantically between the rough waves of the conscious and subconscious, created a haunting, indefinable and hypnotic visual mindscape that we couldn't stop seeing—no matter how hard we tried—long after the film had ended.

—

In March 2015, during the Holland Animation Film Festival (HAFF), I interviewed Rosto for what was to be an edition of *The Animation Pimpcast* series for AWN (it was never published). This interview was made while *Splintertime* (2015), the third part of his Thee Wreckers tetralogy, was making the festival rounds.

—

CR (Chris Robinson): **Where does the name Rosto—or is it Rosto AD—come from?**

Rosto: There's always confusion about my name, but it's all fine because I created the confusion myself. My name is Rosto and the company name is ROSTO A.D. . . . then my production studio is called Studio Rosto AD.

When we were kids, we had funny names for each other. In my case, they put my first name and last name together [for the record, his birth name is Robert Stoces] and it just stuck. I know a lot of these people from those days and they still all have their funny nicknames. Later, I realized it was quite useful. It was memorable and stuck with you. I made an asset of my defects. It had no meaning but I later discovered that in Portuguese it means "face," which is sort of appropriate.

CR: **Can you talk a bit about how you stumbled into animation?**

Rosto: I have been trying to make animated films basically since I was a kid. My dad had an 8mm camera and I was absolutely fascinated by animation and I tried to make my own animation films. I even tried to start my own studio. My little friends had to pay to be part of the studio. This wasn't because of my Dutch entrepreneurship; it was just that it was expensive. We had to buy cels. We had to buy stock. I still have the books that kept track of everyone paying their one gilder (Dutch currency) every week. This was how we bought this stuff. So we were drawing and painting and shooting without any knowledge of how to do it. I have a big box still, filled with failed experiments in animation because it's all out of focus and underlit. I was probably about 7 years old. It was a frustrating business.

When I became a teenager, I was more interested in horror movies. This was quicker and it was more fun to go into a forest with your friends and start shooting. And then it basically disappeared off my radar until computers arrived and I remember doing a quick test on an Amiga computer and being absolute euphoric about the fact that suddenly I could see what I had done. As a kid I could never see what we actually did. The digital revolution was a revelation for me, so I have one foot in the old age and one in the new age.

CR: **When did you make what you would call your first film? Something that satisfied you?**

Rosto: I made a little piece called *Beheaded* in 2000. After so many crappy experiments, this was the first time I felt like I achieved something. HAFF was actually one of the few festivals to select it. It was one of the few festivals that I knew of. I didn't know there was this parallel universe with its own heroes and its own assholes. I was not aware of that life at all. Although I don't see my films necessarily as animation films, it is true that they made room for me in the animation village. Animation is a big part of my films, but not the only part of it. Often I feel that my films are the odd duck in the pond of animation.

CR: **The black sheep of the family**

Rosto: Yeah, which is what I'm used to in a way and I kind of enjoy it.

CR: **Do you cultivate that a bit?**

Rosto: No, it's always nice to feel welcomed somewhere, but you do feel that we speak a similar language but not exactly the same one.

CR: **What about Beheaded was so satisfying?**

Rosto: It had my voice, which was a surprise to me. And I didn't make it to please anyone. I still see young people struggling with that. Not only are they trying to copy other people, they're also trying to please a lot of people, parents, peers etc. These are the demons always looking over your shoulder while you're doing it. You're scanning your brain wondering what this person would say or that person. This is horrible. It's noise. So this was my first film were I was freed from those demons.

CR: **Music is obviously such an important part of your films. When did that interest in music begin?**

Rosto: That happened in my teenage years. As soon as I learned how to play three chords I started a band. I still often feel that energy from starting a band and learning to play. During my art school period I felt this ball of fire while I was playing music but as soon as I came back to art school it wasn't there. When I was head-banging in my room listening to whatever it was, that's what it was all about . . . that passion, that fire . . . somehow it always ended up dead at school. Music is actually the purest way to communicate this urgent and important stuff that we cannot describe.

CR: **When did your band, The Wreckers, start up?**

Rosto: We started that in the 1990s. I had a prog rock project at the time as well. I always think of concepts. I had this almost kind of rock opera thing that I'd been working on and then one of my very best friends—who is the singer for The Wreckers, called Wally, popped up. His voice had developed and we decided that I would play guitar in his rock band and he would sing in my band, which is this complicated opera thing. He wanted to call his band, *The Rockers*, he wanted it to be as simple as possible . . . and then I changed it to *The Wreckers*. We started out by playing noisy cover versions of our favourite songs. It was modern stuff . . . and early stuff like Elvis, the Platters. Everything that we liked. That became more complicated and I took over a little bit and we started to write our own material and that's when the problems usually start.

CR: **What problems?**

Rosto: There's an arc of about 7 years for a band. The guys or girls have to be in their 20s . . . and this is when the magic happens, this is when that fire that we all recognize, that we all love . . . is happening in bands. I think the Beatles are an archetype. It starts with the guys just being in love with each other and out of this love comes all this fantastic noise. Then at one point, life or reality kicks in and it slowly starts to fizzle and usually gets sour a little bit as well at the end.

CR: **What about bands like The Who or The Rolling Stones, who just keep going on and on making inferior music?**

Rosto: They aren't bands, they are brands . . . and fair enough, if people enjoy it, cool . . . but we all agree I think that it's not really what that original thing was. This is why every generation announces that rock n roll is dead. What they're actually doing is talking about themselves because for every generation rock n roll dies. I think *Splintertime* is about that. At one point it's over. You can pretend that it exists or get other pleasures out of rock n roll, which I still do. Music is always one of the highlights for me when I'm doing a film. I enjoy animation the least because it's so fucking slow. It's like euphoria in slow motion. All the other stuff is so immediate and you really get that kick out of it. It's orgasmic.

CR: **When did The Wreckers overlap with your films?**

Rosto: From the beginning. *Beheaded* was a musical short film that was from *The Wreckers*. But in the late 1990s, I started to interpret Wreckers songs for Mind My Gap [a mixed media project that included an online graphic novel series and film trilogy: *Beheaded, (the rise and fall of the legendary) Anglobilly Feverson, and Jona/Tomberry*].

Every song was about a landscape or crossroads and I started to interpret them and this turned into an online graphic novel, *Mind My Gap*. Then I started to use the songs as soundtracks and basically the films came afterwards. It just started to expand from there.

CR: **Do you have an interest in horror?**

Rosto: It's not so much horror, I'm interested in the subconscious. And this is usually where people think that horror starts. If you look at the history of cinema, early silent movies are very often horror movies because it was silent, black and white and very often, shining lights in the dark or in corners. This is why film and animation are so great because it goes into those more demonic areas. And demonic is originally a Greek word not meaning anything evil . . . that's what the Christians did with it . . . because they are scared of all the stuff that happens down there (in the subconscious). Demonic basically just means the deeper waters. And that's what I'm interested in. Because we are so formatted by Christian heritage we often still mistake that for horror or horribleness but it actually isn't. My films are not horror movies. There's nothing really horrible going on.

CR: **Sure . . . but there's a darkness.**

Rosto: I seem to not be capable of escaping this darkness that has followed me around since I was a young man. One of the first things I ever did was a little animation for Sesame

Street and it started, this was before computers, with a smiling, rising Sun . . . and my partner at the time said, "You know Rosto, even when your smiling sun comes up I still don't trust the fucker." There's always something "unheimlich," as the Germans would say.

CR: **Disturbing?**

Rosto: Something like that. It just seems to be second nature. When my films first started to go down the festival circuit I was not aware of this. With *Anglo Billy*, the sun is shining all the time and I couldn't understand why people still called it dark. I understand that darkness isn't necessarily about your colour palette . . . or how much light there is in your films. It seems that my stuff gets on people's nerves. It's very often unintentional.

CR: **Why do you think that?**

Rosto: I don't know. It's just something that is part of my signature, so you just embrace it and at one point you just accept it.

CR: **Did it bother you at some point?**

Rosto: No, I don't think so. It was just food for thought. It just surprised me that no matter what I did . . . . *Splintertime*, I've never made a lighter film . . . and I think its lighter in its subject matter . . . but people still find it dark.

CR: **Well, you have four guys dying in a car crash and a decapitated head.**

Rosto: Yeah, but there's also a sense of humour in it. I mean, *Lonely Bones* was very deliberately dark and uncomfortable. I'm literally quoting from childhood nightmares in that film. So I knew it would be a dark film that possibly nobody was interested in and that it wouldn't screen anywhere and that was all fine. It was just one of those films that needed to come out. That film also makes me feel uncomfortable. I deliberately went to those places.

CR: **Do you still have nightmares like this?**

Rosto: Unfortunately, no, not so much, because I really love them. I am a dreamer. I try to be a lucid dreamer and I have a dream village. When I go to sleep I go to my parallel life and there is architecture there.

I was writing *Splintertime* and we were on holiday in Wales and I didn't know how to open the film yet. One morning I woke up and shot by shot—including the subtitles—I had this dream about the backstage. The only difference was that everything was POV. It was all me floating through the corridors and meeting Wrecker Rooney smoking the snake. Everything was there and it was so fantastic that I have the tools, because explaining it to you or writing it down, it sounds silly.

CR: **But that's always the case. When we share dreams, no one really cares but us . . . but that's because words can never really capture it accurately.**

Rosto: Exactly, because a dream is like water. As soon as you try to grab it, it falls even harder through your fingers. So being able to make it and really find that resonating note—like why this was the coolest thing ever—at one point you find it and you make it like that and I can share it with you. How fantastic is that!? That's the amazing part of the work that we do, that we can literally take pieces of these internal experiences and I can share it with you as pure as possible. Of course, there's still noise. I'm still translating it somehow, but *Splintertime* came so close that I am considering doing something with my dream city [Rosto's final film, *Reruns* would deal with his "dream city"], which is something very concrete and yet very boring to you if I just tell you about it, but it could be interesting to go there in a film.

CR: **Do you keep a journal for writings or drawings after you wake up?**

Rosto: A little bit, but the problem with this is that if I become more diligent about it . . . then I start having dreams about waking up and writing them.

CR: **Do you look forward to going to bed each night? It seems to excite you.**

Rosto: I do. It really does. I just love sleeping and especially dreaming. The problem I have is waking up, because I've been dreaming . . . it's not because I'm tired, I'm just sad to leave that place.

CR: **A few years ago, you made a family film of sorts, The Monster of Nix. What triggered that change in direction?**

Rosto: I had just finished *Jona/Tomberry* and that was a very heavy film. It came from deep inside. I felt damaged.

CR: **Damaged how?**

Rosto: I dunno, I felt a bit raped by myself. It came from a very deep place. We're not professionals. We're still messing with our own psychology and pulling things out, and I felt that I had maybe pushed myself a little bit too hard and too far. It's a film that I'm very, very proud of because it was so honest and I was so hard on myself. I don't think I could do that again now because as you get older, you get more careful.

I wanted to do something light and my son Max was about 6 years old at the time I think. He was my biggest fan. He could give lectures about my universe and explain all the things that the professionals or the academics were still sort of confused about. He was especially interested in these imaginary forest creatures I created. I had many of these stories and I felt that I wanted to make a light fairy tale film for Max. It was also the first film that I didn't make for me because those other films are just works that I wanted to see.

CR: **How was that experience then to make a film for someone else?**

Rosto: I didn't want to write it or compose the music by myself. It was to be a fun collaboration. And then it started and of course everything got very, very complicated. I was in a very difficult period in my personal life. It was almost like the earth was disappearing under my feet. And *Nix* took six years basically to develop and instead of being very light, it became very heavy and I ended up doing a lot myself even though it involved three countries and a big team. I didn't animate a lot myself. I focused on directing. But I did a lot more than I originally planned to do. Throughout those six years the project changed because I was going through this rough patch. We change our minds constantly. Anyway, it became a very different film. It started as a fun little thing for Max then it almost became . . . . it's tough when those rough patches involve a child . . . so maybe this film was . . .

CR: **An apology?**

Rosto: Maybe, or a present. Of course, when the film was finished, he was twice as old and a very different kid altogether. I hope one day he will look back at this film and what it meant to me.

CR: **Some people felt that the film was too dark to be a deemed a family film.**

Rosto: People often say to me that this is not a children's film. I've screened it to many kids and I feel that these people are underestimating kids. Kids are not stupid and too many films insult them by treating them as stupid people. Nix doesn't do that. I used Max a lot as a consultant on that film to see how far I could go. He was very happy to do that. He had a very sharp ear and eye once the film was finished.

CR: **What did Max think of the film?**

Rosto: He gave it, the little bastard, 4/5 stars.

CR: **Did he tell you why you didn't get the fifth star?**

Rosto: Well, he was 12 then and at an age where he is wondering why his dad is so weird. He's 16 now and his peers remind him how cool his dad is, so now I see a reincarnation of feeling a certain pride of his filmmaking dad who has a different voice, but at 12, he was way more sensitive about what other people told him. Of course, *Nix* is a weird film. I thought I really made a family film, but then people start telling me that no, it's not exactly that.

CR: **How do you want to leave your audiences feeling? Do you even think about them?**

Rosto: Hardly because it's noise. You're not honest if you're taking all these things into consideration, which should not be mistaken for disrespecting the audience. That's not the same. After it's done, I'm very, very curious of course to hear opinions because you really hope to find kindred spirits. It's about communication. When I meet people who are moved or touched or interested in the work. When they tell me what it's about, they are usually telling me something about them. This is fantastic. It's like communicating from soul to soul instead of mask to mask.

CR: **And once that film is done and out there, your intentions as an artist don't matter.**

Rosto: Exactly. My job is done. It always feels a bit weird if you have to talk about it or explain it. Most animators are probably borderline autistic. They make films so they don't have to talk about their ideas . . . but once their films do well then you have to talk about them. And all of them feel uncomfortable and shy.

So in that sense I do care about the audience. If I didn't care I wouldn't show them in public.

CR: **In your ideal world though, how do you want them to feel when they leave your film?**

Rosto: Different than how they came in.

CHAPTER 16

Špela Čadež's
Nighthawk

Fʀᴏᴍ ɪᴛs ᴅᴇʙᴜᴛ ᴀᴛ the 2016 Ottawa International Animation Festival to its recent Grand Prize win at the Holland Animation Film Festival, the Slovenian stop-motion short, *Nighthawk*, has stunned and mesmerized audiences and juries with its blunt, tragic-comic depiction of a boozy badger on a blurry drive through darkened streets.

Made by Špela Čadež (whose previous film, *Boles*, also scripted by her writer partner, Gregor Zorc, earned wide international acclaim) and co-produced by RTV Slovenija and Croatia's Bonobostudio, *Nighthawk* is a deeply personal and honest portrait of the destructive, demoralising and pitiful effects that unhinged alcohol feasting can have on a person.

It's an everyday, universal problem that effects far too many people—including the inspiration for the film, Čadež's father. "There was a moment," recalls Čadež, "when we were at my parent's place. My dad was so drunk that he couldn't stand up anymore. He was lying on the floor, and this was the moment where I realized I have to make a film about it, because it was so heavy

DOI: 10.1201/9781003265153-16

83

on me. I had this feeling of, 'I don't really have feelings for him anymore. I don't care if he ever stands up on his feet.'"

What elevates *Nighthawk*—which Čadež spent over a year working on—above many films that deal with substance abuse is Čadež's refusal to judge. In *Nighthawk*, which at times feels like a synthesis of the spellbinding tension *Claude Lelouch's short, C'était un rendez-vous (1976)* with the dirty realism of Charles Bukowski, Čadež creates an impartial snapshot of the waning moments of a long day of drinking. "I wasn't really trying to moralize," adds Čadež, "or to give them any sort of solutions, because I don't have them. I just wanted to deal with a subject that it's difficult for me."

Nighthawk doesn't aim to preach or change anyone. Čadež made the film as a way to navigate through her own confused feelings of anger, devastation, resignation and powerlessness as she watched a loved one disappear.

> I did the film because nobody really wanted to talk about my father's drinking. It's embarrassing. It's something you don't talk about. It's really a subject that is so difficult to start with, and for me, now after this film, it's my treatment, I guess, my therapy.

The idea to use a badger came while Čadež and Zorc were out for a drive and spotted a woozy winter badger stumbling and bumbling along the road. "His belly was almost on the floor," recalls Čadež. "He was so fat that he could hardly move, and we had to stop the car and wait for the 'gentleman' to cross the road."

Later on, Čadež came across a newspaper article about a badger that got drunk and made quite a mess on the streets because it had eaten too much rotten, fermented fruit. Add Čadež:

> What really struck me in the article was when the policeman said that the badger will get in trouble when

he comes home. This was viewed as comic news, and for me, after dealing with my father's problems, I wondered why are we treating drunk people as a joke.

Nighthawk is quite a departure from Cadez's previous films—which were lighter in look and tone and dealt more with love and relationships. One of the most challenging parts of production were the drunk driving scenes—which take up almost the entire film. "I was animating this road for months," adds Čadež, "just this road, and then thinking 'Okay, so now the lights should dance. How do they dance? If I had this darkness and just red spots, what do I do with this?' This was new for me. I usually had a script and then a character has to move about or has to do an acting."

Nighthawk's most significant achievement is the uncomfortable blending of the comic and tragic—which aptly mirrors the contrasting nature of a late night drunk. Let's face it, drunks are simultaneously hilarious and pathetic at the same time. Throughout the film (e.g. the intense high speed drive is revealed through a quick cutaway shot to be sluggish and hesitant), Čadež strikes a unique balance between broad comedy and utter heartbreak. The final scene, in particular, is astonishing. While coldly tossing this pathetic semi-conscious creature to the side of the road, an unseen voice tells a hilarious joke about a drunk man returning to the wrong home.

"That was Gregor who insisted that we end this film with a joke," says Čadež, "because this is the way we want to treat this." Even finding the road to a fitting ending took time.

I didn't really know how to solve all this driving and how to do it with technique. We could not plan the script, because I had no idea how I'm going to end it, so it was sort of difficult to write this, and then to balance this in the studio, how to actually capture this drunkenness. It was sort of a chaotic production.

Though Čadež made *Nighthawk* for her own sanity, it seems to have tentatively had some positive effect on her father.

> I'm not sure what his real reaction was, because he didn't want to see the film with me. He was relieved that I wasn't putting him in the front and shouting, "This is my dad," or whatever. He saw that it's not straightforward. He even stopped drinking for a year.

On the 1st anniversary of his sobriety, Čadež wrote him a message saying, "I'm very happy that you're back."

> I wrote him that, she adds, because he really came back. Conversations with him were there again, and then he wrote back to me, "Thank you, your badger." In that moment, I realized that he really knows that this is me dealing with his problem.

CHAPTER 17

Kaspar Jancis' Motel of Fools

How unbearable at times are people who are happy, people for whom everything works out.

—Anton Chekhov

The really important kind of freedom involves attention, and awareness, and discipline, and effort, and being able truly to care about other people and to sacrifice for them, over and over, in myriad petty little unsexy ways, every day. That is real freedom. The alternative is unconsciousness, the default-setting, the "rat race"—the constant gnawing sense of having had and lost some infinite thing.

—David Foster Wallace, "This is Water"

Okay, calling the characters in the films of Estonian animator, Kaspar Jancis, "fools," might be a tad harsh. In truth, the frequently misguided protagonists of these understated, absurdist, comic-melodramas aren't much different than you me us. They're people trying to figure out their way through this strange fleeting existence.

While Jancis' list of influences include Jacques Tati, Aki Kaurismaki (*Le Havre, Lenigrad Cowboys Go America*), Roy

Anderson (*Songs from The Second floor*) and the "simple" people of Chekov's stories (Jancis admits that few animators influence his work), I tend to see similarities between his films and a couple of contemporary American tv comedies: *Louie* and *Review with Forrest MacNeil*. Both series follow earnest but frequently painful missteps of two protagonists: Louie is a dour, divorced and struggling professional comedian with two daughters; Forrest MacNeil is . . . well . . . how to describe this poor fellow . . . an innocent, bright-eyed and hyper-dedicated host of a TV show wherein each week he enthusiastically reviews real experiences (e.g. addiction, being buried alive, stealing, getting divorced) even as they slowly destroy his life.

Both shows are billed as comedies but in truth they are frequently melancholic as we sit helplessly observing the protagonists (especially poor Forrest MacNeil) make one foolish decision after another. The joy, such as it is, comes from those rare, fleeting moments when something actually (often accidentally) goes—somewhat—right for the character.

Jancis' works are kinda like that: funny on the surface but somewhat tragic at their core. The tragedy, like Review and Louie, stems from the struggle Jancis' distracted characters have trying to connect with their fellow humans. They seem to fear genuine, intimate connection yet desperately crave it. In the Hitchcock-influenced, *Weitzenberg Street* (2002), the man performs an assortment of inane magic tricks to get his lover's attention. Bored, she finds erotic solace in the touch of a mosquito. Touch is all she craves, not tricks. The man finally gets bored of trying to impress her and turns his eyes to another object of desire (a neighbour's fish)—which then leads to secondary storyline about a paranoid neighbour. The woman, now ignored, suddenly craves the man's attention again. Only when the fish and mosquito are eliminated are the couple able to see each other again. Fittingly, the film ends before we see them come together. We are left to wonder if something else will come between them before they reach each other. We see it again at the end of *Marathon* (2006), when a flirting, deceitful (she's part of a gang that is drugging marathon runners, stealing their shoes and then selling them back to them) mother, having forgotten her daughter, races to a playground to find her. As they make eye contact and wave, a train passes between them and leads into the end credits. In the Cartoon d'or winning, *Crocodile* (2009), a one-time Opera star turned boozy, crocodile-costumed kid's entertainer would rather suffer and remain alone than accept an imperfect love (from a woman who owns, for some reason, a pet crocodile).

Even in the more obviously political, *Villa Antoropov* (2012, co-directed by Vladimir Leschiov), disconnect is prominent at a trashy wedding party. When the African refugee arrives at the abandoned party (the groom has, literally, blown up from overdosing on cocaine), he assumes the groom's empty suit and quickly begins chasing the same worthless materialist shit the others were devouring. And what happens? It all blows up. The ending is the beginning is the end for the refugee. All that remains of him and his desire for freedom is a used condom washed-up on the same African shore where he began his futile journey.

Jancis' most recent film, *Piano* (2015) is arguably the only time we get some semblance of a happy ending when the gaggle of disconnected and lonely characters briefly rise above their self-induced miseries when a piano begins playing (triggered only when a tightrope walker apparently plummets to her death and lands in the piano!). For one brief moment, the characters (two of them dead) are aware and truly alive. In unison they gently smile and quietly embrace unfiltered, harmonic joy.

Maybe this is the best we can expect. It's pretty challenging to be constantly self-aware and compassionate day in and day out. Can we ever realistically connect with the world around us for extended periods or are these moments of connection and small joys just fleeting, fading as fast as they appear. Perhaps the best we can do to be conscious and always be ready to recognize those moments of human connection and savour them when they visit.

CHAPTER 18

The Moneygoround

Liu Jian's *Have a Nice Day*

> *Oh, but life goes on and on and no one ever wins*
> *And time goes quickly by just like the moneygoround*
> —The Kinks, *The Moneygoround*

> *It was not this spring morning which they considered sacred and important, not the beauty of God's world, given to all creatures to enjoy—a beauty which inclines the heart to peace, to harmony and to love. No, what they considered sacred and important were their own devices for wielding power over each other.*
> —Leo Tolstoy, *Resurrection*

A slightly different Tolstoy quote from the same novel opens Liu Jian's (who also made the 2010 animated feature, *Piercing 1*) acclaimed and modestly controversial (it was banned from screening at the 2017 Annecy Animation Festival by the Chinese government for reasons not entirely clear) animated feature *Have a Nice Day*, but this quote also serves as a nice summation of this pulp-inspired crime feature that kicks off with a young man stealing a bag of money from a crime boss to pay for his girlfriend's (plastic) surgery. From there, with echoes of Stanley Kubrick's failed-heist

DOI: 10.1201/9781003265153-18

classic, *The Killing* (except those characters had somewhat good intentions)—Jian takes us on a tense and torrid pace following an assortment of feckless, no good people as they menacingly and desperately meander through rainy dilapidated landscapes in search of the bag of money, which they link with freedom and their chance to finally escape their shithole states.

While there are also clear reverberations of Tarantino in *Have a Nice Day* (e.g. hyper violent, overlapping storylines, and a whole lot of happenstance), this is more than an entertaining, turn-your-brains-in-at-the-door caper film. Jian's story is a non-too subtle commentary on problematic aspects of contemporary China, as well as a meditation on globalization, hyper-capitalism and our endless salivation over the promises that cold hard cash offer.

"The movie is set in a town outside a small southern city in China," says Jian.

> And the trends of rapid urbanization and industrializa-tion in the country change a small town like this in vivid as well as in subtle ways. I am fascinated by all of these changes and the people whose lives are affected by these dynamics.

Yet, as Jian, like Tolstoy, cautions that while we can keep on destroying each other and the landscapes, the sun will come up, the seasons will change, the water will flow. All this beauty around us and we just can't seem to see it anymore—as evidenced by the rather startling, serene intermission-like scene of water calmly flowing to open chapter 3 of the film. Echoing the film's Tolstoy epigraph, the river just flows and flows, unnoticed by any-one, except us.

Throughout the film, the characters are engulfed by littered, broken and abandoned landscapes and buildings. Jian nicely uses those images to mirror the inner state of the characters, people who seem without hope, without dreams, all trapped in a hellish cycle that seems right out of Dante. "I use the minor actions and subtle movements of the characters to evoke their emotions," adds Jian.

> Which, along with the vivid landscapes and interiors the characters exist in, constitute the poetic, and in some sense sad and melancholy, aesthetic philosophy of the film. The relation of human beings and the environment is coexistence. Without these people, this specific environment would not exist, vice versa.

The tone of *Have a Nice Day* is equally intriguing with its fusion of relatively simple designs and the blending of stark realism with touches of magic realism: "My favourite artistic style (and in fact my artistic philosophy) is plain and simple," says Jian. The elements of magic realism were born out of, well, reality. "There are so many uncertainties and possibilities to be imagined in such a dynamic and lively space," adds Jian. "What some might call surrealism is often the reality there. In modern China, magic realism is happening around us almost every day. Life at times can resemble a surreal comedy filled with both jubilance and self-paralysis."

Sadly, this daily tragic farce isn't limited to China as anyone living in the UK or USA can attest to during the last couple of years.

Technology also takes some punches in the film. Everyone is glued to their phone, some like zombies. Then there is the character Yellow Eye, who is constantly coming up with new innovations—for rotten purposes. Certainly, Jian seems to suggest that technological reliance has also played a factor in creating this hopeless society. "Everything has two facets," says Jian.

> Even very great things could have side effects. But the level of the side effect depends on other factors. Technology is the same. We need higher IQ to invent greater technological products. But using these products lowers our IQ at the same time.

And despite its sometimes wincing, violent imagery and swift pace, *Have a Nice Day* is an unusually quiet, almost calm film. The silence adds a feeling of claustrophobia and the sense that these people are all trapped in some sort of hell. "I was very serious about the music and soundtracks," adds Jian.

> I would rather not use any music if there is no best fit. Fortunately, we found great music [including two songs courtesy of the Shanghai Reclamation Project, a group that, aptly, combines traditional Chinese instruments with hip hop and electronica). *Have A Nice Day* is the kind of film that explodes its energy in a calm storytelling style with the simplicity of animation film language. Indeed, it was my intention to create the cold but powerful atmosphere.

The downside of the film is that while it succinctly pinpoints many of society's shortcomings, it offers no solutions in the end. Admittedly, there are no easy answers. We have dug ourselves a hole so deep, with systems that we have so intricately attached ourselves. How does one break free of a cycle we are so severely and complexly entwined within?

Jian doesn't know.

I don't know.

But, hey, have a nice day.

CHAPTER 19

Clyde Henry Talks
Gymnasia

GYMNASIA IS A new VR project by the award-winning folks at Clyde Henry (ie. Chris Lavis and Maciek Szczerbowski) who are probably best known for their Oscar nominated, *Madame Tutli-Putli* (2007) and their sardonic trio of short pieces for the NFB's Naked Island series. The project is a co-production between the National Film Board of Canada and Felix and Paul Studios.

What struck me about this VR experience was that nothing really happens in a sense. We're dropped into this rundown school gymnasium. We meet a couple of characters and that's about it. And I don't mean that as a critique of the work . . . it's what makes it so great . . . it's empowering the viewer in a sense . . . it's up to you to determine what it all means . . . they just give you some universal (at least from a Western perspective) trigger points: old school gym, stage, basketballs, overhead projector. I've already seen the project labelled scary. That's nonsense. There's nothing scary about the experience. In fact, it can be quite joyful as you travel back through your own broken memories of elementary school . . . or in my case it reminded me of the last night in

DOI: 10.1201/9781003265153-19

the empty home of my grandparents (the house was being put up for sale) and the many, many memories that a blank wall or a ceiling or a stair projected inside my senses. Watching *Gymnasia* is akin to having a dream . . . you're in the midst of the familiar yet strange and fragmented place and then it just ends suddenly.

CR (Chris Robinson): **What came first? Did you set out wanting to do something in VR or did you have an idea that you thought would work well in VR?**

MS (Maciek Szczerbowski): I don't think it was ever that deliberate. What happened was that we had meet the guys Felix and Paul Studios after we made the stereoscopic film, *Couchmare* (2013).

CL (Chris Lavis): We met them on the stereo film circuit. They were getting into VR and we started talking with them about collaborating on a piece. It was an experiment called Strangers with Patrick Watson which ended up being the first live action VR in the universe. They didn't know it yet but their technology was years ahead of Silicon Valley's. So they had this jumpstart on the technology and took off and worked with NASA, Jurassic Park, Lebron James, Barack Obama etc. . . . We did our own thing for five years and we came to them with the seed of an idea. We had an old idea that we wanted to do stop motion and VR.

MS: There was something that came out of the experience with the Patrick Watson experiment where he looked at the camera at one point and in the 3D experience it was an unbelievably powerful moment. There was a powerful emotional connection with the subject which was something totally other than when an actor looks into a camera during a movie.

CL: We thought that was a worthwhile basis for an experiment for stop motion and see if a stop motion character you shared a space with could create that same intimacy as a human being, which is one of the powers of VR. We set out with that as a hypothesis without proof.

MS: The second weird thing that happened during the Patrick piece was that as he's playing piano and being casual, not acting, he lights a cigarette and takes a couple of drags and then puts the cigarette into a glass ashtray. It was filmed in 3D and 360. When we watched it weeks later in a non-smoking studio space and I swear I could smell the smoke when that happened. Something happened in my brain, on a Radiolab neurological level where the brain was sufficiently fooled by the premise of this being a form of reality and recognized the reality of being six feet away from a burning cigarette. I thought this was cool and worth pursuing. So we wondered if we went into our dusty old sets if we could by a careful orchestration and arrangement of objects and space and sort of poetics that you could maybe smell that part of your childhood: the gymnasium you were in when you were 10 or 11, the weird sweat, the squeaks of the sneakers. Elementary school has a smell, so part of our vein hypothesis was "could we make you smell that?"

CR: **It's scratch and sniff to the next level!**

CL (laughing): We could put gym socks under people's noses while they're watching it.

MS (laughing): You're right, gym socks or old sneakers!

CR: **It's all extended from filmmaker/showman, William Castle, who set up some cinema seats to shake during certain moments in one of his B-movie Horror films. [Later on, Maciek waved an old sneaker around me as I was re-watching *Gymnasia*. I did not notice. Clearly, smellier sneakers are needed.]**

CL: The other thing that's interesting about the medium—cause you said you don't like it and never thought about it much—we haven't much either. People were recently talking about cinematic VR and how film is in trouble, but film is not in trouble. And one of the reasons is because nothing works in VR that works in film. Because you can't edit, you can't lead the viewer's eye . . . so the art of montage is off the table. It's not even the art of storytelling around the campfire because even then you will be compelled to look at the storyteller and if your eyes start to wander that storyteller will bring you back. They'll notice—as they would in theatre—that you're being rude whereas in VR they have no idea. You could be sitting there in a room with Albert Einstein but if you choose to look at the ceiling there's nothing we can do about it. It's a medium where you can't punish people for looking in the wrong direction and that makes it a really limited medium, and for storytelling, almost impossible. But for us, we've never been masters of that kind of storytelling anyway, so it's kind of exciting.

MS: It was a cool experience to not write a story.

CL: What's great is that nobody can write a story. You can set out to make the most commercial VR but there are no commercial tropes. You can't make an action film or horror film in VR. It doesn't work.

MS: There's also no group catharsis. You cannot experience this with people. You're not raised by everyone's laughter.

CL: And because there's no montage, there's not even a moment of catharsis. You can't choose the moment of catharsis. People have then, as we've discovered, but in completely different moments. That's if you're going to have it. Some people watch it and experience nothing. But some people have had a more emotional experience than with anything we've ever done. It's about the experience they had. It's not something where they've been led.

CR: **But you can map out every perspective they could possibly have in the VR experience.**

CL: Yeah, but you can't control *when* they look at something. You can control the space and the sound design and the

sound design probably has more say in story or catharsis than anything. And writing with Patrick Watson
was a big part of it, making him part of the process.

MS: Since we didn't write it and so much came down to being
in time with musical and sound cues, Patrick ended up
becoming a completely valid third writer—in whatever
sense that means—because he determined when and
how things happened and what gravitas they had. The
basketball part was almost completely dictated by his
recording session where he was like a live conductor of
the kids bouncing the basketballs.

CL: Pat did the soundtrack before we animated anything. We got
lucky. I think it's the best thing Pat ever did for us.

MS: The weird thing that we've discovered about music and
sound in VR is that you just watch *Gymnasia* without
sound, time doesn't exist. There's no way to know that
this moment came after that moment. You're not in a
real reality. Time works differently. Music is the only
way to make you think time is moving forward.

CR: **Why did you choose a school gym?**

MS: We do a lot of stuff with local French experimental theatre.
Their specialty is site specific theatre where the audience might be driven to a forest or a cemetery. They said
to us that when you're doing site specific theatre and
you're choosing that space you're choosing your main
character. As a director you have to be careful to not
come in with a full dialogue, maybe you have half of it,
because you don't want to drown out or ignore the other
half of the information that will come from the space
itself. Let the space speak.

CR: **And that's what happening in *Gymnasia* where the gym
is in fact the protagonist.**

MS: Exactly. Our thinking was something like: which part of our
collective memory is the dustiest in your memory bank.
We've been in classrooms since we were young. We've

been on buses or walked in hallways. They've been refreshed so the old ones are gone, but the elementary school gym is a place we rarely revisit.

CL: . . . and if you do, the scale is completely different. They're much smaller than you remember.

MS: You're not in sneakers . . . you didn't just pee yourself. You're not in that moment at all.

CR: **I don't recall the peeing part.**

CL (laughing): Neither do I.

MS (laughing): Oh, I do!

CL: They're really interesting spaces. They're ritual spaces. You go to Christmas concerts and magic shows. You play in them. That's why we put you on the stage so that you get that feeling of what it's like to be a kid again.

MS: It's a kind of ceremonial space and it's also a repository for an entire dimension of your childhood that you haven't revisited. It's also universal. I had that experience in Poland, Chris had it in Toronto. A large amount of people will likely feel it's their gym.

CR: **The experience really does rely on say, a good viewer.**

MS: To some degree . . . even if you decide to stare at the corner ceiling I think there's still some pleasure.

CL: you can't control it and it's really interesting. You end up with a ratio of every 10 people, 2 or 3 will be completely unmoored. One out of twenty gets really emotional and some of the rest think it's really cool.

MS: Some think it's creepy.

CL: What's kind of nice, unlike short films, is that you get a sovereign experience. You're not in a program of 40 films. You have your little moment with this.

MS: And if you go back in a second time, it will be different. There's no way you can have the same attention to the same things with the same timing.

CL: I wonder if people are more honest in their reaction at the moment they remove the headset, compared to watching a short film.

MS: And how comfortable they feel being watched while they do this.

CL: We don't really know yet because it hasn't become public. Right now people are watching it with us there and they take the set off and here we are acting like puppies: "What did you think!? What did you think!?"

CR: **I wonder how kids will react. They're still in that space.**

MS: We'll have our Radiolab moment at Tribeca, so we'll see. I mean, some people have cried. I don't know how comfortable they are crying in public.

CL: I wonder too how kids will react. My daughter is that age but she doesn't want to watch it. And how will it play in other cultures? We think its universal, but when someone in China watches it will this feel like a Western gym?

CR: **There's something almost anti-climactic about *Gymnasia*. I was waiting to be scared or shocked by something. So it's like nothing happens yet it triggered all sort of memories and emotions for me.**

CL: The end is abrupt because we ease in like a dream and end abruptly.

CR: **When I thought about it after, I remembered my grandparents place being put up for sale. I remember the last night in this empty house. I'd be looking at a blank wall but seeing all this stuff from the past come alive.**

MS: Memory doesn't actually seem to be encoded in your head as much as in the places where they happen. When I go back to Poznan, I remember stuff that I am unaware of here. It's inaccessible to me. If I touch this fence or am next to that fountain, I remember that moment, but the memory is in that fountain or that fence. Otherwise I feel like I don't have that memory anymore. And I think that's something we were trying to do, to get your "access denied" memories.

CR: **I had hoped for some liberation for the viewer in VR, but most often I still feel I'm being led and controlled.**

CL: Yes, but you know what's interesting, *Gymnasia* has worked most powerfully on people who are cynical about VR or haven't watched a lot. The hardcore people have big ideas about interactivity and being able to grab things.

MS: And we didn't want to do that. We wanted to have a sort of dream anxiety. You want to run but you can't. You want to stand but you can't. Am I small in this space or big? These are questions you don't normally ask yourself in real life. But the idea of not being able to move and having the whole scale fuck up of being in a puppet world, but on their terms, I think that contributed to that kind of dream anxiety.

CR: **The little boy and the overhead lady character both look like standard old dolls.**

MS: There was something by the poet, Rilke who had this idea that there is a powerful relationship between us and dolls and puppets because we had them when we were babies, tiny children . . . it was through these objects that we invented our own adulthood. When you watch kids punishing a doll they are applying an authority that they don't have with us, with their parents. This is their training ground for becoming an adult. Secondly, and I think this has a lot to do with the feeling of *Gymnasia*, is that kids at that young age use these primitive little dolls to invent death or their understanding of it. Sometimes our first understanding of death comes through puppets or dolls. You grow up and throw them away but on some visceral level you associate them with childhood and death.

CL: and by the way that's what Toy Story is about. Every single Toy Story is about death and aging.

MS: This is the first film in animation where we didn't make our own heads. Normally we scalp our puppets. The idea here was that because of the Rilke theory, we didn't want the puppet to be *that* boy, we wanted it to be everyone's dumb old puppet, the most average puppet head you could find.

CR: I know you don't like hearing that *Gymnasia* has a creepy feeling—at least initially. I didn't feel that the second time around, but I think that those generic looking dolls do trigger a feeling of creepiness. I don't have an abundance of childhood memories, but one of the strongest is an encounter with a kid's Raggedy Ann doll. It scared the shit out of me. And the fact that some 5 decades later I still vividly recall this shows you how powerful that experience was.

CL: The creepiness is important. The director of *Missing Link* was saying something recently that puppets don't have to be creepy. I think he was wrong, like epically wrong. And Cartoon Brew had the story about how Missing Link bombed and in the comments part there were some people saying . . . "Time to get back to *Coraline*." And I also noticed that my 9-year-old daughter and her friends all talk about *Coraline*. It's not just that it's a scary film, it's a growing classic. And at some point you have to admit that the medium has some of that DNA in it. It's like stop motion has two siblings: one is Aardman and one is creepy. It doesn't seem like you can go in between.

CR: **Could you achieve what you wanted to do here within a short film?**

MS: No. We'd have to command the camera. We'd have to show you what's behind and when do you show you that. I honestly feel that when I ask you sit down and watch this, it's not like a film, it's more like, "Hey Chris, did you see this garden behind the studio? Why don't you check it out and walk through it." And that's it. It's over. And maybe you'll want to go visit the garden again and you can, but it won't be the same because you'll pay attention to something different. And that's not the same thing with a film. A film is not a walk through the garden but a walk through the garden is a cool experience. I think that's where Pixar fucked it up. Story story story and nothing other than story. And VR is not for that.

CL: There's an interesting essay from the guys from Story about why story doesn't work in VR. They call it the "Swayze effect." It's by an ex-Pixar guy part of this thing called the Story Studio. He says that VR experience where characters are interacting and things are happening without the acknowledgement of your presence . . .

MS: Makes you feel like Patrick Swayze in *Ghost*, where you're like, "I'm right here! Why can't you see me?" And people are walking past you and through you.

CL: And probably the most powerful moment in *Gymnasia* is when the boy looks at you. This is not the Swayze effect. It means you are on stage with the boy. Then you start asking yourself, "Why am I on stage?"

CR: **Yeah, I thought the kid was going to knife me.**

MS: I remember your reaction verbatim. You suddenly said, "WHOA! Who the fuck is this guy!?"

CL: You've watched thousands of short films and you have probably never once said that. It also means, conversely, extreme limitations. If you have an idea for a short story that involves story, for god's sake don't do it in VR.

CR: **Will it be disappointing to go back and do a short film?**

CL: I don't think so.

MS: Listen, drawing is still fun. Finishing a draw is still very satisfying.

CL *(laughing):* I think the most disappointing thing now would be if we were forced to do another VR piece. We're actually making a very traditional short film next, with dialogue. The challenge is that it's 3 acts, dialogue, virtually no surrealism. It's like our version of *The Straight Story* [David Lynch feature film]. It's very traditional, really old school. It's a nice way for us to return to puppets.

MS: It's an experiment for us because we've never done that.

CHAPTER 20

The Crushed Dreams of a *Magnificent Cake*

> *"I do not want to miss a good chance of getting us a slice of this magnificent African cake."*
>
> —King Leopold II

It's a tad early to begin making bold predictions, especially given the unpredictable nature of festival jurists, but for my money, *This Magnificent Cake* by Mark James Roels and Emma De Swaef (*Oh Willy . . ., Fight*) is one of the finest animation films of 2018. This complex, multi-layered 45-minute work is set in the late 19th century during Belgium's colonization of the Congo Basin in West Africa. Divided into five chapters, the experience and effects of colonization are shown from a multitude of perspectives: a king (based on Belgium's King Leopold II), slaves, a crooked, drunk businessman, and an army deserter.

This Magnificent Cake is an astonishing, sensitive and original stop motion work that eschews time and subtly drifts between

DOI: 10.1201/9781003265153-20

reality and illusion as it explores the crushed dreams and lives caused by the disastrous, brutal and inhuman effects of colonialism on both the innocent and guilty, and the good and the awful. With dashes of magic realism, Roels and De Swaef place us in a sort of dreamscape where we're never quite sure where we are, and never quite sure if what the characters are experiencing is real or not. It's wonderfully disorientating.

"I don't really remember how or when we came up with the idea," says Roels,

> but I do remember both of us really getting into *Journey to the End of the Night* by Céline and being inspired by that. In one chapter the main character meets a black servant sitting in the kitchen of a manor making bombs. In another chapter, the main character describes going to an African colony to work and how terrible that was. The one idea that stuck with both of us was that it was nearly always the very worst individuals that Europe had to offer who ended up going to these colonies.

While two chapters focus on utterly devastating experiences of slaves, the other storylines are tragic in different ways. One involves Van Molle, a baker who has fled to Africa with the profits from his family's bakery. The other follows Louie, an army deserter who escapes to Africa to avoid enlistment or prosecution. "The two storylines," adds Roels, were initially going to be part of one story in which a young Belgian in colonial Africa is terrified by the very imposing and promiscuous behaviour of his next-door neighbour. Many drafts later, this next-door neighbour with his odd habits and excessive drinking morphed into the character of Van Molle, the shady baker. Writing the film, we went through so many different iterations we sometimes wonder if one of those drafts lying somewhere in a drawer is the real gem and this is just a meek compromise. As Emma often says, "Did we get off one stop too late?"

The decision to make an anthology film came quite late in the pre-production process. In early drafts of *This Magnificent Cake*, Roels and De Swaef had no specific storylines or consistent characters. "It was supposed to be a fragmentary portrait of a period and setting," says Roels. "Then we realized we were getting stuck and actually really missed following characters through a longer narrative. Right up until the start of the shoot we were cutting out characters and settings, some of which had already been built (e.g. a manic Jesuit, a bereft ape). We wanted to find a good balance of drama, comedy, tragedy, absurdity and plain stupidity which might have felt a little too much for a single narrative to handle."

For those familiar with the duo's previous work—the widely adored and acclaimed, *Oh Willy . . . .* (2012)—their distinctive "windy wool" look will be instantly recognizable in *This Magnificent Cake*. The materials enhance the oddly dreamy and realistic atmosphere of their work. "We try and use materials," adds Roels,

> That walk the fine line between revealing what they are and creating the illusion of something completely different. Most things are pretty obvious, there's a lot of wool and fabrics involved. We travel around a lot to find the right materials, a clearance sale of Flemish velvet in Roubaix, alpaca wool from Manchester and horsehair from the horsehair capital of Rennes.

Working alone on any film obviously has its own share of challenges, but undoubtedly a collaboration could potentially create a unique series of obstacles (administration, organization, egos). Not so, it seems, for Roels and de Swaef. "Writing and developing is always a long period of brainstorming together," says Roels.

> During production our roles are kept pretty separate. While Emma oversees set construction and puppet making, I'm mostly gathering reference material and working

on the shooting storyboards (these are storyboards that are actually useful during the shoot instead of the impossible flights of fancy of our initial boards). During the shoot I am also not too involved with the animation, mainly keeping busy framing shots and lighting sets while Emma and her team set up the decors.

One of the most striking aspects of the film is the subtle and pleasantly minimalist use of sound and music. So many films—animated or otherwise—too often rely heavily on music and sound to inspire emotional reactions in an audience. In *This Magnificent Cake*, the quieter moments (whether it's a slave speaking to a decapitated head of a friend, a servant bathing the king after he's pissed himself, or the extremely touching, albeit bizarre, moments between the drunk and a snail, or the tears falling from the face of Louis' father's) generate tension and, more often, compassion for this sad lot of characters. "We're very finicky about using music," admits Roels.

Finding the right music is always a long drawn out process that usually takes months of listening to various things. Every now and then a certain piece of music will transform the scene and that is the best feeling. The film is actually pretty dense in terms of sound, our sound designer Bram Meindersma was constantly running out of the amount of layers he could use in his software. There's a lot going on in those quiet moments.

CHAPTER 21

The Frog, The Dog and The Devil

The Ballad of Bad Whiskey

YOU DON'T HEAR IT so often these days, but there was a time when "getting lit" meant drunk. Not sure what the etymology is, but I imagine it's connected with fired up, and alcohol being a temporary cure for inhibitions. Lit might even connect to enlightenment though I don't recall any such occurrences during or after the many benders I've forgotten. Regardless, lit up is an apt description of *The Frog, The Dog and The Devil* from New Zealand animator, Bob Stenhouse. Getting lit isn't just what the boozy protagonist does during a wild bender, the term also reflects the film's glow-like look.

The story was inspired by *The Devil's Daughter* (sometimes known as *The Godley Ghost*) an old ballad by New Zealander, Ernie Slow. Stenhouse was first introduced to the ballad by a colleague at the New Zealand Broadcasting Corporation (NZBC).

When Stenhouse later moved to the National Film Unit (the New Zealand version of Canada's National Film Board), he proposed making an animation short based on *The Devil's Daughter*. Stenhouse believed it was an ideal story for animation because "the ballad was a rollicking good yarn, plenty of action, allowed considerable impact in experimental visual effects and sound design and was New Zealand material."

The story itself is quite straightforward and actually fairly removed from Snow's original ballad. One night, (a Friday the 13th, to be precise), a shifty drunk tricks a tavern barkeeper out of a bottle of whiskey. As he sneaks his way out into the night, the man drinks down the whiskey and stumbles, slinks and skitters through a hellish hallucinogenic bender shared with she-devils, demon dogs and other unexpected encounters. It's the bender of all benders. By night's end, all he's guzzling is a jug of water and momentarily breathing in the gospels of teetotalism.

So, yeah, the story itself is fairly familiar. Sort of a Sleepy Hollow meets Kerouac. What really makes the film stand out is Stenhouse's extraordinary visual effects. There is almost a neon-like glow throughout the film. The lanterns, lightning, puddles, water reflections—seemingly minor aspects of the film—become supporting characters owing to Stenhouse's breath-taking paint with light approach.

"The glowing halo 'neon' effect," says Stenhouse,

> —multiple film exposures on opal glass, sandwiched between layers of underlit artwork—was being used by local television graphic designers at the time for programme titles and promos, and I wondered if the same effect, "painting with light," could enhance a whole short. As well as adding a "photographic" appearance to the artwork—hard to achieve by hand—it also made quite simple shapes look much more complex.

Now, back in those days before digital technology ran the world, it would take a hell of a lot of painstaking work to achieve this lit look. Because Stenhouse was shooting what he calls an "artwork sandwich" using top-lit and under-lit art, he had to do multiple passes ("roughly the equivalent of a feature," he says) under the camera. This meant that once he'd shot the top-lit work, the camera gate would be closed, the film rewound and then exposed again with the under-lit art. Stenhouse guesses that he sometimes needed up to twenty additional passes of the same film through the camera for the most complex shots.

The complexity of this process led to an assortment of problems for the camera operator. To the point where Stenhouse took over the camera because "it was easier to shoot it myself rather than write instructions for someone else to follow. I could also make demands on myself that I wouldn't ask of someone else."

The slightest fuck up would mean re-doing days and days of work.

Outside of the audio, Stenhouse did the whole project (storyboarding, artwork, painting, backgrounds, shooting, editing) himself. He estimates that it took him about two and a half to three years to complete.

The Frog, The Dog and The Devil was an instant hit on the festival circuit taking Grand Prize at Canada's Hamilton International Animation Festival (where the OIAF temporarily relocated to in 1986) along with an Oscar nomination for best animated short. "To win Grand Prize was an immense honour, and validation of the work that had been done," says Stenhouse,

> but really, it was not until I was invited to Hiroshima 90 as one of the judging panel, along with John Lasseter and others, and saw Alexander Petrov win Grand Prize with *The Cow*, that I did appreciate, with some envy of course, the acclaim I had missed by not being able to attend the Festival in Canada.

In 2000, *The Frog, The Dog and The Devil* was selected as one of the 84 (no, I'm not sure why they chose 84, maybe it's an Orwell thing?) best animated films of the 20th century.

Interestingly, Stenhouse had no knowledge of the work of animator, Don Bluth, whose animated feature film, *The Secret of NIMH* had some visual similarities to *The Frog, The Dog and The Devil*. I wondered if it frustrated Stenhouse to discover this after devoting so much time and energy to his passion project: "No. It felt good to have produced a short that compared in some ways with the "latest" major feature release, especially when half the population of California seemed to be in credits of *The Secret of NIMH*."

CHAPTER 22

Consuming Chris Sullivan

THREE TROUBLED AND unhappy individuals living in a dour, industrial American town connected by a dark past. With themes of mental illness, spirituality, abuse and addiction, *Consuming Spirits* isn't your typical animation film, and Chris Sullivan isn't your average animator.

Sullivan's films (e.g. *Master of Ceremonies, Landscape with the Fall of Icarus, The Beholder*) show us a world neither heroic or beautiful, nor exceptionally ugly or evil. Sullivan's working-class characters struggle daily against poverty, abuse, death, madness, want and despair. But Sullivan is no preacher or social activist. His blunt, bare and unpretentious films aim, not to shock, but to engage us, to simply show us a world that most of us deny living in.

Fourteen years in the making, Sullivan's *Consuming Spirits* focuses primarily on three characters: Earl, Genny and Victor. Earl hosts a late-night radio show on gardening where he frequently escapes into musings on existence and morality. Genny drives a bus and takes care of her ailing, foul-mouthed mother. Feckless Victor works for a newspaper and struggles with alcohol

DOI: 10.1201/9781003265153-22

addiction. The three characters don't realise that they are all connected by mysterious events from their past.

Consuming Spirits shifts between past, present and imagination. The past is often conveyed in sketchy, ink-on-white, drawn animation. Sullivan also uses still photographs along with model and cutout animation. The latter techniques give the film a heavy, lumbering atmosphere. The town is dark, gloomy and stagnant, littered with dead trees. The characters are awkward, plain and frail. They look as though they might fall apart in an instant.

As with Sullivan's short films, the characters here are neither good nor bad. Their faces are tired and beaten, eroded by failure's dust. They are confused, myopic and haunted people, struggling through life until something happens to shake them from their waking sleep.

CR (Chris Robinson): **What was the starting point of Consuming Spirits?**

CS (Chris Sullivan): The roots of this film have several starting paths that converged as the film developed. I come from an alcoholic family, and a family with lots of social service intervention. Including temporary foster care. My father was the lone alcoholic, so it has not become pandemic, amongst my 10 siblings. Which is a blessing.

So that is where much of the "plot" of the film comes from. But there are other important images, a Shaman exhibit in Chicago's field museum shows a Manichean in a Haida Shaman, the description on the display describes a romantic view of an alcoholic and I thought it was interesting to imagine how premature death canonizes you in some ways.

CR: **Did you always envision *Consuming Spirits* as a feature?**

CS: Yes I did, I had some early notions of it being episodic, but as I began to make the film, no cliffhanger or semi closure moment emerged. I also thought of it as 90 minutes not 128. My ideas in performance and writing were just stretching out, and the animated short did not fit into my brain anymore. I don't think of making features as some sign of artistic maturity, it's just where my work was going.

CR: **How does the final script compare to the first script?**

CS: The early script was much more ironic and used film noir tropes. Victor and Genny were the main characters and Earl was the outsider, and kind of the villain. He made moonshine in a dry county (Allegheny Mist), but he did have a gardening show.

The development of Earl's voice becoming the hub of the film is the main change. I found the most freedom writing his material, and part of that was that as a radio personality, his language was somewhere between conversation, and oration, a place I like. Gennie's section with the little foundling was also a pleasure for the same reasons. There are many scenes in the film that were in the very first draft. Other scenes like the confession scene were written in the early to mid 2000s.

CR: **Why did you decide to use cut out animation? It seems to be a perfect choice since your characters are quite fragile and awkward . . .**

CS: The initial reason was because I knew there was going to be a lot of language, and the possibility of drawing all that dialogue seamed gratuitous.

But as I started to make the characters, the possibilities of colour, and environment became apparent, and the stain of everyone and everything became very interesting for me. I very much liked being able to trust my animators to make a scene work. And that happened more easily with puppets.

CR: **Although there's an abundance of music in _Consuming Spirits_, it's primarily as part of the character's performances. You rarely use a score, instead trusting the viewers and your imagery. Few filmmakers, let alone animators, these days have that sort of confidence.**

CS: The music in *Consuming Spirits* was always part of its fabric, but actual sound track moments are more than one might remember as often there is very soft music in the back: Victor visiting asylum, Earl's confession, Genie's foundling scene, Campfire with Earl. But the performed music of the characters I think works better with some non-musical elements around it.

CR: **How did you fund the film?**

CS: I received money from the Guggenheim Foundation, The Rockefeller foundation, and I am blessed with a full time Job at The School of The Art Institute of Chicago, which allowed other expenses in my life to be taken care of.

CR: **Can you talk about writing and your literary influences? Your writing always stands out.**

CS: Language is where my films start, though I am an animator.

There are both writers and filmmakers who have really made me have bravery to do what sounds stupid in one's head. Dennis Potter, is a huge influence, also the radio artist Joe Frank. *The Singing Detective*, and *Rental Family*, are my two favorite pieces of art. RD Lainge, the poet Galway Kinnell, Ellis Peters, Joyce Carol Oates, Jeannette Winterson and Julian Barnes are other influences. I also collect educational and medical archaic texts, which come up in a lot of the awkward signs and formal dialogue. The *Encyclopedia of Sex*, and *Psychiatry for Nurses* are two of my favorites.

CR: **There's an underlying . . . actually . . . at times an overwhelming pessimism in your films. People live in this frequently disengaged world and a lot of crappy stuff happens to them. There is a tinge of hope at the end of *Consuming Spirits* but it's hard to celebrate given the weight of tragedy that has already befallen the protagonists. Are you really this cynical about society, about life or are you just a realist?**

CS: For me there is a kind of catharsis that I think suffering brings. When I am making my work I sometimes do feel like I am being ruthless, and that it will be a hard pill to swallow, but I also appreciate so much when artists do this in their work. I want them to leave me hanging, strip me of comfort and closure. Leave me out in the cold. It is what Mike Kelley once referred to as "negative Joy." I am a softy though and cannot tolerate a total abyss. I do need some survivor, some glimmer of hope somewhere in a piece of work. I also think that truly evil people are pretty boring, and I am very angry at the over representation in media of for instance serial killers. Let's say there are 300 serial killers on this planet, and think of the amount of media time, and media attention they are given. Pure monsters. They bore me. I am much more interested in the little monsters and angels that are inside most folks.

CR: **There's always this sense of instability and fragility in your films. We never quite know where we are or who we're watching. Your characters seem to drift in and out of the present, future and past. Either they're remembering or imagining something. Your characters seem to struggle with being in the present, in the moment.**

CS: In many ways the characters in my film are very different from me. I can be in the moment, and live it. They are like me in that they are not cruel, but they are reckless through ignorance, but even more so through their limits. They want love, belonging, and a sense of accomplishment, but they just do not have the goods. The shift in tense is something I have always loved. I also think that a survived event is very different than one you are in the middle of, and I like to make that point of survived and present blurry. And I do disagree with Proust that the past is past.

CR: **I can't think of anyone to compare you to in animation: you're one of a kind. Still, you're an animator for a reason. I wonder why you choose it as a way of expressing yourself, and if there are animated films or animators who've had an impact on you?**

CS: I think my individual quality is that I fell into animation as a craft I can do well. So wanting to make important films is definitely a stronger urge than wanting to make great animation. (Opportunity for heckle!) I use humour, but I never think "I need a gag here" or even need a stretch and a settle.

Historically, there've been many other animators who've made strong films in experimental forms: Jan Svankmajer, the Brothers Quay, Priit Pärn, Igor Kovalyov, Paul Fierlinger, and more recently Don Hertzfeldt, Emma de Swaef, Marc Roels, Jérémy Clapin and Janie Gieser, to name a few. Seeing Piotr Dumała's live-action film *The Forest* is amazing. He's doing with live action what he does with animation and primarily without language.

CR: **You're already at work on a new film, right?**

CS: *The Orbit of Minor Satellites* is a project funded by Creative Capital.

This film will be a feature as well. Some ask me if *Consuming Spirits* is a hard act to follow, and I say no. It gives one faith when their strange and awkward Frankenstein monster reaches people. To be given audience is a blessing, I hope I have let it all out for my viewers, and it is a renewable resource. There is a lot more to come. Will just have to stay alive, and do it.

CHAPTER 23

It's a Good Life, If You Don't Weaken

Luc Chamberland and Seth's Dominion

Seth's Dominion (2014), Luc Chamberland's loving and mesmerizing portrait of the world of the acclaimed Canadian cartoonist, Seth (*It's a Good Life, If You Don't Weaken, Palookaville*), is a fascinating exploration of the artist's complex world; one that is nostalgic, sad, and yet somehow hopeful and inspiring. Skirting between live action interviews and animated recreations of Seth's work, Chamberland takes us inside the artist's creative process (and astonishing productivity), while giving us hints of a man seemingly still struggling to make sense of a somewhat fractured childhood and a past that no longer is, and perhaps never was. Seth's beautiful, detailed art seems to be his escape, his sanctuary. It's as though he didn't like the world he was given so he just made up his own.

DOI: 10.1201/9781003265153-23

But *Seth's Dominion* isn't only about Seth.

In his introduction to the beautifully designed book and dvd edition of *Seth's Dominion* (which includes a short *Making of* along with two shorts based on Seth's stories, *The Death of Kao-Kuk*, *The Great Machine*), Seth serves up some interesting insight: "I saw the film several times. While watching it . . . something occurred to me. In some way . . . the film was more about Luc . . . than it was about me."

"It's true that this is my vision of him," says Chamberland during our recent chat in Montreal.

> A different person would have done a different film. It's a film about my sensitivities about life. I see the angst in Seth's work. I related to his characters. I wanted to talk about life and how we should take things and find sweetness. I saw it underlined in Seth's work. I took advantage of his work to talk about things that interested me.

And when you learn that Chamberland spent seven years working on *Seth's Dominion* (almost like a hobby, he says), you begin to understand what Seth means. "I was teaching part time in the mornings," he says, "and then after I would head to the NFB and work in the afternoon until early evening." During those years, he also worked on a TV Show (*Wild Kratts*), made an animated documentary short (*Saga City*, 2011) along with an assortment of commissioned works. "Everything I was doing was for Seth," adds Chamberland.

> A lot of the money I made for those projects went into the film. Usually I had to balance at least three things at once. This is why I use notebooks so that I organize these different projects. This doesn't include travelling to Guelph, Ontario, Toronto and New York to conduct interviews for the film.

While many viewers are convinced that the animation segments in *Seth's Dominion* were hand drawn, in fact only three scenes were done on paper. The rest was made on a computer. "I would prefer to do it on paper," says Chamberland, "but budgets are so small that it's just impossible now. I like to have something tactile, having the artifact in your hand, getting your fingers dirty."

In fact, it's rare to run into Chamberland without pens, pencils and notebooks alongside.

> Wherever I travel I always have pens and pencils in every pocket and small books with squares layout help me making frames for scenes compositions, a small in my jacket pocket, a medium in my bag, and a big one for home so I'm always ready to jolt down the to many ideas that attack my head.

> It's very neat that I draw on the Cinétique tablet, but it's weird for me because it feels like it doesn't exist, though I know that it does exist as a film. I really worked hard though to make people believe it was all done on paper. We scanned old paper to get textures and I worked really hard to get a brush that looked like it was inked by hand. I did a lot preparation on thumbnails and I did nearly all layout on paper and then I scanned them and put them on the Toon Boom "Animate" software.

Although he has worked on many commissioned projects during his career, Chamberland admits he found the task of adapting Seth's distinct retro style cartoons to animation stressful. "I was very scared when it was time to show him the first animation. I worried that he wouldn't like it."

Chamberland found the pacing a couple of ways. First, by observing Seth's movements during their interviews: "I saw," adds Chamberland, "a strong, quiet tranquillity inside of him that I wanted to emulate." Secondly, he asked Seth to record the narration for every animation short used in the film. "That's when I found the rhythm. Music is very important for me and I didn't have any music . . . so his voice became the music in a sense."

Chamberland didn't need to worry. "The second that Seth saw the animation he was smiling and happy. He was almost honoured that it was well done. And like that, all my angst vanished."

From the beginning, Chamberland had carte blanche with the film. "Seth was clear that he wanted me to have complete freedom. He doesn't like being told what to do and wanted the same for me." The only people who did take Chamberland to task were NFB folks. He originally envisioned a film that was broken into small parts.

> I had an elaborate synopsis but I was told that it was too confusing and needed to be more linear. The situation reminded me of Oliver Stone's *JFK*. He constructed the film in the same way, but was told to make it more linear. So he rewrote it like that, but in the end he cut it the way he wanted. So when I was asked to make it more linear, I smiled and agreed and then I broke it back apart when I made the final cut and everyone said it made sense.

I wondered what were some of the biggest challenges Chamberland faced—other than keeping focused for seven years—approaching a subject who mostly just sits in his basement and draws.

> When I had the initial idea for the film, I wondered who's going to see this and how can I make it interesting? I'm a bit of a film buff and so I watched a lot of films about cartoonists. The two that helped me a lot were *Crumb* and *American Splendor*. I didn't want to do a film about a guy talking and drawing. I wanted to do a film about life and the subject matter in Seth's books.

While the bulk of Seth's work carries an underlying sense of loss, alienation and anxiety, Chamberland uncovers the hope and joy within that deceptively gloomy vision. He does this not just through his re-interpretation of Seth's world, but through the never-ending flow of positive energy and excitement he brings to the film. You can feel Chamberland's love and admiration dripping through every frame of the film, not in some salivating fan boy manner, but with a profound respect and empathy. Both artists remind us that *this* is all so fleeting and that we have to put aside our fears and unhappiness, that we can take control of who we are and how we choose to live.

You'd be hard pressed to find many artists these days who would be so devoted to a project for a couple of years, let alone seven, but Chamberland never lost sight of where he was going.

> I was very focused. I look like a person who is all over the place. I have pens in my pockets. Notebook in my bag. Notebook in my pockets. Notebooks everywhere . . . there's too much stuff happening in the head so I write it and write it and get it out. The more I do that the more it seems to control it. I put it on paper there so I don't have to think about it. It's there.

In this age, or, hell, any age, how can someone be this consistently optimist and happy? (Let's not forget Chamberland's loud, boisterous laugh that is recognizable to anyone who has been in a room or cinema with him!) "I look like a happy go lucky person," he admits to the surprise of no one.

> I impose happiness daily and hourly. I find that extremely important because the angst I have inside is killing me. So I am really disciplined about imposing fun in every endeavor. I want everything to be a great experience and life is short. My daughter is severely handicapped. They told us she wouldn't live past four. We had a little cry, say twenty minutes. Then we said, let's make sure she's going to have fun. We made every day happy. Now she's 18 and she's still happy and keeps having fun. A state of mind helps everything you do.

CHAPTER 24

Yield by Caleb Wood

CALEB WOOD IS ONE OF the most energising and inspiring new indie animators on the festival circuit right now. Since graduating from the Rhode Island School of Design, the Minnesota animator has made somewhere in the range of a dozen experimental films incorporating an array of techniques and themes.

In 2012–13, Wood was in Japan for a residency (he eventually made Goodbye Rabbit, Hop for the programme). In his spare time, he photographed avian anal street stains. Wood then animated each piece of white shit into Bird Shit, an ingenious abstract animation that at one point fuses the individual droppings together to form a single flying bird. Top that, Mr. McLaren!

Last year Wood made about half a dozen films, all worth seeing, but my favourite is Yield, his unofficial follow-up to Bird Shit. This time Wood uses roadkill as his inspiration. A slew of ex-animals race randomly by until one magical point where— look closely—a stunning regeneration occurs as the carcasses seem to claw, walk and run towards rebirth . . . until a final shocking image puts a halt to any and all dreams of immortality.

"I've been compulsively documented instances of death for a while," says Wood,

DOI: 10.1201/9781003265153-24

but without any conceptual goal. After I made Bird Shit it hit me that I could reassess my impulse to document death through animation. The ultimate goal would be to bring life back into death, to create movement from documentation of life's final poses.

It took Wood two weeks of driving around Minnesota state roads to collect the roadkill images. "I drove around in a circuit twice," Wood adds, "mainly on county roads. Sometimes I'd find something on highways, but those situations are much more dangerous in terms of other drivers, and I'd have to pass them by. There's not one person who won't say 'what the fuck?' and get distracted to some extent when they see you photographing dead animals on the road, so I tried to keep observers to a minimum. Cops also have no problem pulling over to ask you questions, and can be pretty difficult to convince."

If I saw a tuft of fur, circling ravens or even dark red skid marks, I'd pull over and document the scene with my camera phone. I never touched, moved, stepped in or interacted with the dead animals in any way, other than capturing what I saw in photos.

In just under two minutes, Wood has created an ingenious work that reminds us of the frequently violent and callous way— in life and death—that we treat animals, and a stark reminder that our own existence could be as fleeting and forgotten as roadkill.

CHAPTER 25

Visiting *Ville Neuve* With Felix Dufour-Laperrière

THE CANADIAN ANIMATED FEATURE, *Ville Neuve* will not challenge *The Avengers* or even *Missing Link* at the box office, and that's perfectly alright. Eschewing the frequently mindless excess, racket and predictability of mainstream cinema, Felix Dufour-Laperrière's intimate and poetic hand drawn film (made with 30 people, a budget of $1.6 million Canadian dollars and using about 80,000 drawings all made via brush and pencils on paper) takes place during the turbulent, anxious times of the 1995 Quebec referendum on independence.

Set in a calm coastal town on Quebec's Atlantic Coast, *Ville Neuve* fuses personal and collective destinies through the ruptured lives of a family: Joseph, a bitter hard drinker; Emma, his ex-wife, and his estranged son, Ulysses.

While *Ville Neuve* is set during a divisive time in Canadian history, the film also reflects today's increasingly fractured state of affairs.

DOI: 10.1201/9781003265153-25 **127**

*CR (Chris Robinson): **Ville Neuve** is a very quiet film and yet there's an enormous amount of emotion and tension that is still conveyed. Can you talk about your approach the sound design/music? Many animators today seem scared to rely upon their images and story and too often seem to drown their film (like they do in Hollywood) in music and sound/noise.*

FD-L (Felix Dufour-Laperrière): It is indeed a quiet film. I wanted to play with density, both visually and with the soundscape. *Ville Neuve* tries to put in resonance the intimate and the collective. In order for these echoes to be heard, it needs to have some space and length. Visually, figures and objects are often isolated, taken apart from their context and then established as symbols or signs. It leaves a lot of space for the sound, which is used both for giving context and information and for its own textures, for the sensations it conveys. As the dialogues and monologues are central to the film, the composer (Gabriel Dufour-Laperrière) and the sound designers (Olivier Calvert and Samuel Gagnon-Thibodeau) worked with various intensities, for the words to be audible and to sustain the length of the shots, to link distant spaces and suggest the connections between each character and between the individual desires and the collective ones.

In animation, the reality we represent is never far away from the artificiality of dreams, desires, intimate images we carry within ourselves. I like to establish these spaces as connected, very close to one another. The sound allows to open paths, to overlap these spaces.

CR: **How long did you work on this? How challenging was it to stay focused on such an ambitious project for a long period of time?**

FD-L: The first lines of the script were written in 2012 and the film premiered in 2018 (in Venice) and is being released in

Quebec and France this spring. It is quite challenging, over this long period of time, to keep our will lively to make a film, but the making of the film was an adventure in itself, an adventure that was shared with a wonderfully devoted team. Making a handmade film, with a pretty restrained budget, working on paper with a light and flexible production structure pushed us to reinvent our tools, to revisit our visual and technical approaches. In the end, it was a great time, yet exhausting.

CR: **I'm curious about the origins of the film. Did you have a plan that you want to try a feature or did you just have a story in mind that you knew had to be a feature?**

FD-L: I was wishing to make a feature, but a feature that would keep a part of the grammar, the independence and the flexibility of the short form. Animation, in my eyes, is at its best in independent short films, where we can feel that it is invented during its making, that the searching goes on, where we can feel that something is found in the very process of making the images. It allows a real freedom and a very powerful cinematic toolbox.

The story itself was freely adapted from a very short story from the American writer Raymond Carver. I took the general context from his "Chef's House," the energies of the characters, and transferred them to Quebec, within a very specific, and tensed, political time.

CR: **How much of the film changed over the course of the creation/production?**

FD-L: Visually, quite a lot. We've had the pleasure of trying various transitions, visual approaches and rendering of the "reality" of the film. Yet, the final film is very close to the script. Even with the desire to maintain a real freedom and leeway with mise en scene, the script often seems the only object of stability within the turmoil of the production!

As the budget was limited, I've done a year and a half of preproduction, drawing all the key poses and preparing all the shots to be given to animators. It gave us a certain latitude in the production itself to readjust some shots, framing and editing. And to animate some parts with an important part of improvisation.

If the film was in part precisely scripted, it still had certain spots of total liberty. For example, the scene where Emma reads a passage of her book to Joseph wasn't detailed in the script. The text was, but all the images that emerge from the darkness were created afterwards, with the pleasure of having a moment of pure moving drawings.

CR: **What was it specifically that sparked you from the Carver story?**

FD-L: I was moved by the two main characters, who convey opposite yet complementary forces. The man is submerged by fatality and anger, but he is still alive and full of desire, an idealist maybe, in a dark way. The woman is lucid yet in resistance. She maintains a challenging sense of hope, without illusions but with a necessary determination. I felt that the situation of this couple gave a light on the Quebec political situation and that it would easily be translated in this different context.

CR: **Were you certain there would be no colours in the film? Did that make it even more challenging given the overall quietness of the film?**

FD-L: The black and white was chosen at the very beginning of the writing. For its graphical quality and for the possibilities of superimposition it allows. The shades of grey permit, maybe more than colour or maybe with a greater readability, transparency, blending and overlapping of images.

It was also a choice of working with ink on paper and to achieve quite simply a specific graphic signature. But the next film (*Archipelago*, an animated documentary), will be very colourful, I kind of miss vibrant colours and tones.

CR: **I loved the scenes where we see the ocean reflected in the cabin window as the couple are talking. It really creates this sense of entrapment, maybe also of hope as well, and just how thin that line is between hope and despair.**

FD-L: You totally grasped the intention of these scenes. The sea is at the same time a threshold, an opening and a limit, the end of the land and a space of possibilities, a horizon.

For this scene, the man, woman and sea were animated on different layers. We've mixed them quite simply, dealing with transparency. This is an example where a certain minimalism becomes a strength. The space of the cabin is rendered with only a couple of details, the reflection is a frame within the frame, the white of the paper suggests a depth that we don't need to detail. It allowed us to easily combine the animated layers.

CR: **The background characters (e.g. when Emma and Ulysses have left the cinema) are in stark contrast to the black of the main characters . . . they're almost transparent . . . ghostly . . . like they don't matter in the world of these somewhat ego centric protagonists.**

FD-L: Collective existence is always partly an abstraction, a combination of elements of various densities and opacities. I wanted the crowd to be at the same time undefined and more than the addition of individuals. The combined transparencies of the bodies build a new whole, that exist by itself but that don't always interact directly with the protagonists. The crowd then has a graphic existence, its own space and territory, that overlap, superimpose or is hidden by the main characters. Yet their shades enlighten the protagonists, they draw their attention. And at the end, one of these dark figures, on the top of the church steeple, is revealed to be the son, Ulysse.

CR: **I found it quite surprising how much of the complaining by the protagonists is directed at their fellow French Canadians. I guess that my being an English Canadian, I always thought the dislike/frustration was directed towards the Anglophones.**

FD-L: Who loves well, criticizes well, I guess . . . . Seriously, I feel that the question of the independence of Quebec isn't to be thought with frustration over the Anglos or even the historical inequities of the Canadian federation. It is more a matter of self-determination, of a collective will, of common desires and freedoms. We've said no twice to the possibility of our independence, so the responsibilities are ours. As are the consequences and the actual political disappointments.

CR: **A lot of that bitterness towards fellow Quebecois comes from the father and son, yet it seems to me that—at least until the bell has rung in the final scene—they are equally guilty of the complacency they accuse others of.**

FD-L: Totally, they are definitely a part of what they condemn. It is maybe the origin of their worries, their bitterness. As it is part of a lucid way to conceive politics. We're always, in various way, part of the status quo. And it is confronting our desire for change.

CR: **The link between the bell sequence from Andrei Tarkovsky's film *Andrei Rublev* (which Emma and Ulysses watch together in a cinema) and the final scene of *Ville Neuve* (where, after Quebec votes to leave Canada, Joseph rings the church bell as his son watches) suggests that there is hope for not just Quebec, but also the father and son.**

FD-L: The son and father meet under the bell in a partial moment of unity, in a moment of shared individual and collective existence. Their difficult relation is for me echoing the challenge of establishing continuities, of dealing with filiation and the passage of time. Of embracing change, acknowledging its promises and origins.

CR: **Given the events of Brexit, do you think Quebec separation is still possible anymore? Even if the Yes win, there seems to be no guarantee that it would lead to a separation (as we are seeing in England right now).**

FD-L: The independence option remains relatively strong, with an important popular support. The political vehicles that carry it aren't, however, in a good shape. And they are very divided. A future referendum will certainly not take place in a near future. That said, our collective existence remains to think and organize. To dream. And future political and ecological turmoil will certainly bring to the forefront the issues of the French language, the challenge of living together, the redistribution of wealth, the preservation and occupation of the territory. We will be confronted, as a small nation, with the same challenges as the big ones. With the limited means that are ours. The desires for independence, as much from the gigantic American neighbor as from the actual Canadian federation, could well make a comeback. But as you said, nothing is guaranteed. There is the Brexit on one side, with its confusion. But we can also look toward Scotland, that will probably plan another referendum, on a very different basis then the Brexit.

I'm a bit pessimistic but I feel that we're obliged to maintain the reflection, the will, the difficult hope.

CHAPTER 26

Where Is Here

Felix Dufour-Laperrière's Archipelago

IT'S ONLY BEEN TWO YEARS SINCE Canadian animator, Felix Dufour-Laperrière, debuted his critically acclaimed animated feature, *Ville Neuve (2019)*. Incredibly, he's already back with an equally multi-layered, mesmerizing and innovative new feature, *Archipelago*, which is all set to debut at the 2021 Rotterdam Film Festival.

Framed by the voices of an unknown woman (she might well be the voice of the river or mother nature or Quebec) and man (who frequently tells her "you don't exist"), we travel along the Archipelago of Quebec, passing by many islands on the St. Lawrence river that make a large chunk of the Canadian province. Along the way, we encounter various sights and sounds from Quebec's real and imagined past. Memory, history and dream are all rolled into one, just as they are in our daily lives, even if we're not always cognizant of that (e.g. I look at family home movies and they don't jive with my memories of some of those people and places and temperaments).

DOI: 10.1201/9781003265153-26

More visually and technically diverse and ambitious than *Ville Neuve*, *Archipelago* (which was made half on paper and half animated with TVPaint or under the camera) incorporates a number of impressive animation styles (courtesy of a couple of dozen animators including Malcolm Sutherland, Philip Lockerby, Jens Hahn, Eva Cvijanovic) and techniques (drawings, scratch, paint, pastel, collage, stop motion, rotoscope) in addition to manipulated live action and archival scenes.

Made over a period of three years (the core part of production was completed just before the Pandemic greeted us) with a team of 12 animators and a modest budget of $625,000 (Canadian), *Archipelago*, is a poetic, personal and political work that plays with word, image and sound while circumnavigating a real and imagined collective and individual history,

Archipelago is an intentionally restless film. We're never quite sure where or when we are or who is speaking (akin, undoubtedly, to what some Québécois—and even many Canadians—feel about their fractured history and identity). The freewheeling and fragmented narrative mixed with the diverse, and often rough, drawing styles gives the film a sketchbook diary sensation, as though Dufour-Laperrière has cracked open his head and invited us to rummage through the assorted discoveries and impressions.

·

CR *(Chris Robinson)*: **Given the short time between Ville Neuve and Archipelago, I'm guessing you had this new film planned and scripted before Ville Neuve was even finished.**

FD-L *(Felix Dufour-Laperrière)*: I started writing it in 2015 just a bit after the script for *Ville Neuve* was done. Honestly, it was a gift. It was fun to write. It was very close to me and it was easy to finance, which was surprising given the "experimental" approach. It was damn fun to make. It was the kind of film that I wanted to make when I finished University but I didn't have the money or maturity to be able to organize it. I just wanted to go inside a studio with people I like to work with and make images for two years. That was really the basic principle.

CR: **How was that different from the process of making Ville Neuve?**

FD-L: With *Ville Neuve*, I was trying to control more. I did all the layout and key frames myself. I might have tried to control too much. For *Archipelago*, it was fun. I only made some image, notes, excerpts and from these references, the animators would go off on their own for six months and we'd talk every other day or so.

CR: **In some ways Archipelago feels like an extension of Ville Neuve, except you maybe move more away from the personal towards more abstract and fragmented perspectives, as though you're merging all kinds of voices from past and present into a single narrative.**

FD-L: It's a bit of the same subject matter, treated differently. Formally it's very different. Lots more colour. I wanted to get away from the grey of *Ville Neuve*. I wanted to have fun. It's a film about what makes a home or territory but I was putting a lot of things that I love in the film from Quebec writer, Hubert Aquin, to my grandmother and daughter. When we belong to a place or a community, country or family, it is real but there is also an imaginary dream space, something that you project onto that space. So there is a concrete part but also an imaginary aspect. That is precious to me.

CR: **Yes, it seemed to me that while you certainly explore Quebec and this idea of, as a character says in the film, an "impossible province," you are asking a more general question about what is home, what does "home" even mean.**

FD-L: Exactly. *Archipelago* has the same political intuitions as *Ville Neuve*, but it's treated differently. A lot of it came from the relation with the archives. We love old footage of, say, windmills. It's loveable. It's also false, imaginary and a politically problematic view of the past. Archival images can be sort of beautiful. You feel like a kid, like memories of childhood.

CR: **That's so true. Every so often I will go onto the National Film Board of Canada website and watch some 1940s or 1950s films about, say, Ottawa. There's something comforting and warm about these works even though they're complete bullshit. Home movies are the same way. Everyone looks so jovial and loving and united in them, but the everyday reality was quite a bit different.**

FD-L: Yes, absolutely, they're false. It's theatre.

CR: **We're also never quite certain who is speaking, let alone where and when those voices are from.**

FD-L: That was intentional. It's linked to home, to something we belong to being part real and part imaginary. When we observe a situation, there's a lot of real and imagined past that goes into our present perspective. It's like a post-modern take on history. Everything is contemporary, past and present are living together. For me, it's pretty important because it helps you name things that you feel and perceive.

CR: **Did you spend a lot of time rifling through archival footage?**

FD-L: Looking for the right archives wasn't painstaking, rather an on-going process during the whole first year of production. Some of it was planned to be included at the very beginning, others come from family footage, friend's film (actual footage and b-rolls). Some of it was shot in 16mm during the production (but appears as "archives").

Surprisingly, the principal archive footage that is used to, in a way, structure the film (The islands of the Saint-Laurent, with the maps and footage from the 40s), wasn't planned. I found it while looking for other material.

This archive is used in various ways: as a quotation (giving images and words from the past), as a basis for the rotoscopy, and also "against itself," meaning it is reworked and edited to criticize itself, to reveal that a part of it is false, politically oriented and that we can (or should) also take a different meaning out of it, so that a different historical narrative can emerge.

CR: **What does that phrase "impossible province" mean to you?**

FD-L: It's Quebec's political destiny. We are still in this limbo between being fully part of Canada and carving out our own destiny. Many do not accept Quebec fully being a province of Canada. There's this unresolved tension. Jacques Ferron [a Quebec writer and doctor who is referenced in the film] had a phrase the "uncertain country," so it's parroting that a bit.

CR: **I sense that you would like to see Quebec be its own nation, but do you also feel frustrated over this indecision . . . like "Can we just make up our mind? Either we're going to be part of Canada or and we're going to form our own nation."**

FD-L: Yes. I think we sometimes have this grocer mentality where we calculate the advantages and disadvantages. That thinking just doesn't shape a political destiny, so yes I get frustrated that we can't seem to grasp something.

CR: **You could say this about Canada as a whole. It's always been this uncertain nation where we frequently ask: Who the hell are we or more famously there's a quote by Canadian scholar, Northtrop Frye, "where is here?" Are we English? American? Where is this thing called Canada?**

FD-L: It was a surprise to me that the same uncertainty is shared in English-speaking Canada.

CR: **Because of the experimental or non-linear approach and the different styles of animation, it sometimes felt**

like being inside someone's sketchbook diary. Was there a lot of improvising going on?

FD-L: Yes, a lot. From both me and the team. The team was really generous and involved. They had a lot of freedom but they gave a lot of themselves. There were 5–6 people who spent the whole two years with us.

CR: **Did you ever have any moments, because you were improvising, where you thought, "shit, where is this going?"**

FD-L: Yes, every week!

CR: **It must have been liberating too.**

FD-L: Yeah, it was good to just step out of your ego and not try to be so controlling. It was fun to talk with people you like being with and to see the images they'd made. I did a feel a bit of anguish though about not having a film. I'm very precise with the editing. I recorded and edited the dialogue at the beginning so it's very clearly placed. And I started putting the images over that. There was over twice the dialogue originally. So it was free yet precisely framed on the editing line.

CR: **How did you settle on these animators and what instructions did you give them?**

FD-L: It varied. For some sequences I was quite precise, but for others I gave them brief notes and then just say, "go and draw like you draw." So your impression of it being like a sketchbook is right. Jens Hahn did some of the crowd sequences. It took me two years to convince him to just "go ahead man and do what you do." I knew he was a painter, but he never shows anyone his work. He's really good at free drawn portraits so I just asked him to do what he does. I had some ideas about what I wanted for certain scenes and approached animators whose work I thought would fit that. For example, I asked Phil Lockerby to draw the scene where people are drunk because I knew he was good at sketching people in bars.

CR: **What's next?**

FD-L: I have a new feature that is written and partially financed. It's a French/Luxembourg co-production called Death Does Not Exist. It's a tragic take on political violence.

CR: **Do you set out now to make a feature or do the concepts dictate that?**

FD-L: (laughing) It's a bit of pride perhaps, but I do love having a screening to myself. It's wonderful. I love the length and space that you get directing a feature. You can take more time. It brings animation out of its normal public. I appreciate that. I've often launched films in a non-animation context. Those audiences often seem surprised by this auteur side of animation and the beauty and strength of it.

CHAPTER 27

Laughing at Chaos

Alex Boya Talks Turbine

Aᴸᴇx ʙᴏʏᴀ ɪs ᴀ ᴍᴀɴ ᴏꜰ two worlds. Although he was born in Sofia, Bulgaria, on the heels of the collapse of the ruling Communist Party, he has lived in Montreal since his family immigrated when he was two years old. So, on one hand he carries what he calls "dispersed letters, objects and old photos of a time just before my birth," yet he's also a typical North American child whose closest experience of conflict was playing with *Star Wars* toys.

This border straddling existence has given Boya a more detached perspective on the complexities of his roots in Bulgaria and global conflicts in general. "I totally miss the human tragedy. I only know the toys depicting soldiers, that's the lottery of time and location."

These two disparate worlds meet in Boya's latest short film, *Turbine* (2018), a comic techno soap opera about the effects of war and technology on a married couple, produced by Jelena Popović at the National Film Board of Canada (NFB).

"It's weird," says Boya, "in that sense because *Turbine* clearly shows eastern Europe, but then you have a western nuclear family

DOI: 10.1201/9781003265153-27

143

unit and some of the American dream in the appliances our protagonist so tenderly loves. I guess I'm from both worlds."

Both of Boya's parents are artists, so it's not a big stretch to understand how he developed an interest in art. "Like many kids," says Boya, "I discovered Crayola in kindergarten and never stopped drawing since."

After studying illustration and design at Montreal's Dawson College, he was briefly enrolled in the acclaimed animation program at Concordia University where he made the short film, *Rites of Passage (2012)*.

"Where I really got influenced," adds Boya, "was when I was hired by McGill University to produce medical illustrations (and other instructional media) for several internal communication departments. Doing those kinds of drawings has always been my thing since I was a teenager."

Boya's first contact with the NFB came in 2015 through the studio's acclaimed apprenticeship program, *Hothouse*. Under the tutelage Oscar winning animator, Chris Landreth (*Ryan, Subconscious Password*), Boya was part of a group of 8 directors who were challenged with producing a one-minute film in three months. Boya's contribution was *Focus*, a stunning and imaginative attempt to visualize attention deficit disorder that earned him an Honourable Mention for Best Canadian Animation at the 2015 Ottawa International Animation Festival.

"The idea," notes Boya, was to make "a documentary" by revealing the mental convulsions of an animator that does not focus on what he should animate on paper. My motivation was then to maintain the spontaneous nature of a documentary with finely calculated drawings, with as much photo realism as possible in the context of a 3-month project."

Fittingly, given the fusion of an almost taciturn, medical precision with vivid, manic drawings in *Focus* and, later *Turbine*, Boya has defined himself as a medical expressionist.

It is a conceptual approach that seeks to define intangible states of the soul with the clinical definition of a physical representation of medical visualization in the traditions of renaissance drafts of the inner body. In addition, it plays with the instructional undertones of images to animate anticipation of meaning and inner conflicts within the mind's eye, as more freely demonstrated in *Focus*.

That same year, Boya approached NFB Producer, Jelena Popović, with an idea for a film that explored Post-Traumatic Stress Disorder and the rise of technological dominance through a married couple. Production started a year later.

The roots of *Turbine*, oddly enough, don't come from experience, but from a dream. "I dreamed of a wide field and a man's back," says Boya.

> Turned closed enough to profile his face, I saw it was flat. When I faced him, there was a turbine in the hollow face. Saliva/engine oil drooled; he told me to get closer to whisper in my ear. Everything in his mechanical rhythmic voice was deeply understood. Awake, however, I realized it was just the bedroom air conditioner.

Though the time period is not defined, *Turbine* is clearly set during the aftermath of a major war. Yet, Boya's concern is less with war on a battlefield than with the subtler conflict that unfolds in domestic spaces. "The battlefront is the initial recalcitrance," says Boya, "but its products seep into the household in subliminal technocratic dominion in the form of mundane appliances and eventually as appendages of the body.

While it might be more obvious to focus on something contemporary like smartphones and the internet, Boya wanted to go back further into the past to examine how war birthed these technologies. "The smartphone is too implicit because it's a slick impenetrable capsule containing "magic." Go back a few cycles, though, and the home computer is clearer opened layout, with a keyboard, a screen, an energy source, etc. Return a few loops even further and you can find a plane, a turbine and also the war that kick-started these technologies."

While technology is central to the film, *Turbine* also touches upon the shock of war on individuals.

> Our pilot's emotional luggage is essential to the plot. It is a romantic tragicomedy about a husband whose body merged with his warplane. Due to having an airplane turbine instead of the face, he can no longer communicate with his wife. She attempts to gather the fragments of their life, and that's where the theme of PTSD comes in.

The resulting work is a rich and multi-layered work that leaves us to consider many issues, predominantly, our overreliance on technology, outmoded gender roles and, naturally, the often unseen horrors of war.

Oh . . . and don't fear these complex and scary themes, *Turbine* is also . . . well . . . it's a very funny and surreal soap opera about a messed-up guy who falls in love with a ceiling fan and the absurd lengths his wife will go to preserve their marriage.

Sometimes, all we can do is laugh when chaos engulfs us.

CHAPTER 28

Banana Skins and Cigarette Butts

The Films of Adam Elliot

"Men are so necessarily mad, that not to be mad would amount to another form of madness."

—Blaise Pascal

"Insanity is relative. It depends on who has who locked in what cage."

—Ray Bradbury

"People often confuse me, but I try not to let them worry me."

—Mary and Max

Adam Elliot's claymation films polarize me. On one hand, I occasionally cringe, and tense up while tasting his sentimental narratives with their, at times, cloying, pathos-drenched narration and sad, big-eyed and doomed misfit characters. The cynic in me thinks of Faulkner's iffy relationship with race and questions the authenticity behind Elliot's sentiments. Is Elliot really seeking to "normalize" his afflicted characters by shaking up our stale,

DOI: 10.1201/9781003265153-28

stigmatized perceptions of those with mental health issues or is he a cinematic snake oil salesman putting his Aardman-esque "wonders" on display at a pity party carnival beckoning one and all to "Step right up and get your ticket to see these marvelous wonders of humanity!"

On the other hand, I find Elliot's detached and unassuming portraits refreshing and illuminating in their simplicity (even as it agrees with "first hand" that the ham narration of the short films verges on the burlesque). Elliot deftly takes an animation technique that has largely been associated with the slapstick feathery silliness of Gumby, Californian Raisins, Celebrity Deathmatch, and a daft old British wanker and his dog—and uses it to construct thoughtful personal and poetic portraits of normal people with somewhat unusual traits or interests.

All of Elliot's protagonists have some sort of affliction (e.g. cerebral palsy, Tourette's syndrome, Asperger's syndrome, Asthma, OCD, Testicular cancer, alcoholism, mood "disorders"—an unfortunate term) but it does not define them, it is simply one of their many ingredients. There's an uncle who enjoy crumpets, tea and urinating on a lemon tree; a young cousin wears a superhero outfit, has lots of pets, collects things and has enormous strength despite a paralyzed arm; an older brother has asthma, an eye problem and a slew of adventures. Harvie Krumpet likes to touch people with his index finger. Harvie works at a dump. Lives life through Television. Gets punched out. Metal plate in his head. Fired from many jobs. Gets struck by lightning. Heavy smoker. Gets ball cancer. But he keeps on . . . keeps surviving . . . falls in love, joins a nudist colony, adopts a flipper girl who adores him. Wife dies. Harvey ends up in a home. Befriends another guy, Hamish. They bond and behave like teen twits. Then he dies.

Is Harvie's existence really so pitiful or is it a life like any other? He had love. He loved. He was touched. He touched. Seems to me that Harvie lives life fully. We should be so lucky.

Then comes beautiful dear ol' Max, Elliot's finest achievement. Society says that Max is mentally ill and has Asperger's Syndrome among other things. Max, though, doesn't give a damn what he's called. As he bluntly tells Mary after reading her book on Asperger's, "I do not feel disabled, defective or that I need to be cured. I like being an Aspie. It would be like trying to change the colour of my eyes." Max is not more or less content with life than the rest of us. Okay, he freaks out when he gets stressed and stands in a corner. Stressed people frequently turn to drink, drugs or any number of escapes. Max's reaction is no better, no worse.

Max eventually forgives Mary with wise, tender and surprising insight: "You are imperfect, and so am l. All humans are imperfect."

Elliot does not judge, mock or humiliate. He simply offers us people as they are with all their wonderfully unique diverse eccentricities. Elliot is asking us, "What's the big deal? We all know people with unusual quirks and traits. Hell, we ARE those people." That's kinda the point me thinks. How can there even be other when we are they?

What does it even mean to be different, defective, to be mad insane afflicted eccentric odd unique unusual or "quite the character"? Aren't we just attacking what being human is all about? And who decides, defines what is normal? Is it those with an already fragile sense of self? If we designate other and difference, we can maintain the fantasy that we are somehow whole. Cognitive apartheid.

Can there even be a fixed normal? That suggests that identity/self is stagnant and unchanging. We've become a society of label makers. Everyone has one. Everyone has to have one. We're dangerously obsessed with mental health these days. Gone are the days when someone was an eccentric, a loner, a thinker, a downer, quirky, or simply just "a character." We replaced them with machines now. Spectrum, personality disorders, bipolar, anxiety. Everyone is welcome. Room for all. No one is left out. Pills for any occasion. Difference is mouthed but not spoken or heard. We talk so much about tolerance and acceptance of other as we become more intolerant than ever. Don't do this, can't do this. Kids can't be kids anymore. Don't fit drug them. Muffled by overactive fear-mongering. People can't shout smoke drink fight. No right turns one way street don't talk back books books books experts consultants all telling you me and them that they're wrong everything they do is wrong unless they do what they do a society of crippled children stunted at birth growing into ninny know it all parades pressure pressure pressure to be RIGHT to be NORMAL to NOT MESS UP self help you help me help help this says that says this which is what is which wich witch PRESSURE TO ADAPT AND FIT TO THAT THAT EVERCHANGES We said don't drink this now drink it Eat this NO DONT. People talk as if there is a way one-way good way only way. There is a way, your way. Only way all the ways making us sick turning us into selfish arrogant intolerant lapdogs wagging and running wherever their told EVERYONE MUST FIT FIT FIT FIT FIT.

It's MADNESS!

And where are we with it all? Are we better? Are we smarter, more informed? No no no. Plato wrote about that cave . . . always that damn cave . . . the one where he said people spend their lives, where they never actually step outside and see the WORLD as it IS FACE TO FACE MONO A MONO STEP OUTSIDE OUTBACK FIGHTING WORDS None of that only shadows, we only encounter the shadows of things never THE THINGS THEMSELVES TV TV TV INTERNET FACEBOOK TWITTER MOBILES ALL THE SHADOWS OF THINGS NOT THE THINGS THEMSELVES We don't have friends anymore just Facebook friends. Don't speak just tweet. SO MUCH HAPPENING THAT IT OVERWHELMS makes you mad if you don't tweet or Facebook you're odd or worse you're a phony a faker snob just avoiding it to be show you're better.

We've gone beyond Plato.

We've reached a stage where we don't even see ourselves anymore.

Until we accept our perfect imperfection, we'll continue to destroy each other and ourselves.

To paraphrase Max, people might confuse and confound you, but try not to let it worry you. Just worry about yourself.

In Shakespeare, it's always the fools who are the wisest. Max is no different.

> When I was young, I wanted to be anybody but myself. Everyone's lives are like a very long sidewalk. Some are well paved. Others, like mine have cracks, banana skins and cigarette butts. Your sidewalk is like mine but probably not as many cracks.

It's not Max, Harvie, Mary or your moms, dads, brothers, uncles or cousins who are the misfits, but you . . . me . . .

. . . us.

. . . together.

CHAPTER 29

Pineapple Calamari

GRIEF IS NOT FUNNY TO the grievers, but I'm sure it can seem pretty absurd to onlookers.

After a close friend died, I inherited his leather jacket. I wore it often, imaging it was keeping him close to me, almost like his arms were protectively wrapped around me. I'm sure it seemed to those around me as touching and strange as it now does to me in memory.

Such stories abound, of course, but *Pineapple Calamari*, a painfully hilarious take on loss that's partially inspired by Christopher Wood's painting *Zebra and Parachute*, is among the most memorable. Kasia Nalewajka's National Film and Television School grad film is how one imagines a collaboration between Hitchcock and Aardman Animation might shape out—dressing the creepy, fetishistic leanings of *Vertigo* in *Creature Comforts*-style clay animation.

As in *Anomalisa*, the use of stop-motion animation creates a distorted realism, a "kinda-lifelike" vibe that suggests an emotionally damaged holding pattern, a denial triggered by despair so enveloping that reality is cast aside (by both the woman and the horse). Yet—again echoing Vertigo—reality is askew here even before the tragedy. There is an unreal, dream-like quality to the

DOI: 10.1201/9781003265153-29

setting. Who are these women? What is their relationship? Why all the rum and frogs? Why is the chicken such an ass?

It's such a surreal situation to start with that you're left wondering, especially with the comic twist at the end, if what we're viewing isn't itself the product of a damaged mind. But whose? The grieving woman's? Her late partner's? The horse's? The chicken's?

Does it even matter?

The end result is a beautifully crafted, original and paradoxical work that takes us deep inside the paradoxes of the human unconscious, where reality and impossibility rest comfortably and logically together, like a horse in a dress.

Even though my friend has been gone for almost eight years now, once in a while I put on his coat, certain that I can feel his presence. Pain's volume lowers with time, but never entirely goes quiet until we do.

CHAPTER 30

The Joys of Jodie Mack

F ILM STRIPS, weeds, concert posters, maps, boarding passes, jewellery, photo negatives, envelopes, dollar store gift bags, beads, books, blankets, puppets, floral patterns, fabrics of all shades and colours, computer memory boards, junk mail and even a horse's kidney stone. All stuff you might stumble upon in a bizarro garbage heap, not animation films. The ultimate recycler, experimental animator Jodie Mack, animation's Dr. Frankenstein, finds beauty and repurpose in life's leftovers as she breathes new life into the forgotten, discarded and unconventional. Mack's collages clash and collide along the way towards a sense of harmony and unity.

With rapid fire creativity fueled by unfettered delight and rampant curiosity, Jodie Mack has created an eclectic body of work that bridges contemporary art and animation with an utterly unpretentious—to borrow from music—lo-fi, D.I.Y. approach.

The comparison to music is not random. If there is a common thread between Mack's films beyond the obvious unharnessed joy emanating through every frame, it's music.

DOI: 10.1201/9781003265153-30

> A lot of shorter films that I have are kind of secret music videos for these songs I was really into at the time. I always joke that I make films, but I really just wish I was a musician. And I actually do, but a live musician. Not someone that needs to worry about the recording. But someone that just like performs!

Mack's passion for music seeps through every pore of her work, whether it's straight up music videos (e.g. *A Joy, Twilight Spirit, August Song, Curses*), musical documentaries (*Dusty Stacks of Mom*, which features Mack's playful and eclectic interpretation of Pink Floyd's *Dark Side of the Moon*), or animated musicals (*Yard Work is Hard Work*). Mack sings or performs in a number of her films. She's performed both *Dusty Stacks of Mom* and *Unsubscribe #4* live, and her short, *Rad Plaid*, involves live audience participation.

It will then surprise no one reading this text that music was Mack's doorway to art. "I loved to learn things on the keyboard by ear as a kid and I really got into singing as a child," says Mack. After her family moved from London, England to Florida, Mack became involved in choirs and performing arts at school. While Mack's passion for singing was strong, she didn't pursue it professionally because of the often suffocating "rules."

> Singing was fun until you want to do it for real and then it's like you can't smoke, you can't cry, you can't yell, you can't do anything fun. And you just have to really live a different lifestyle than I was headed for I think.

After some interest in theatre (which occasionally incorporated silhouette and cut-out animation), Mack took Film and Media Studies at the University of Florida. One of Mack's teachers screened the likes of Len Lye, Norman McLaren and Harry Smith and encouraged experimentation. "We had access to some old 16mm films that we would soak in bathtubs full of bleach and experiment with," says Mack.

My first point of entry into the idea of animation really was a painterly one. I thought of the film strip as a canvas. I'd work on the film strips sideways and then all of the sudden you put it another way and you see all the individual frames. You're just fumbling around chasing your tail until it makes sense. And there were definitely a lot of discovery moments that way.

After graduating with a BA in Film and Media Studies, Mack headed to the Art Institute in Chicago for Graduate Studies. There, she encountered animators Chris Sullivan and Jim Trainor. Oddly enough, Mack didn't take any animation classes in Chicago.

I was a teaching assistant for a couple of classes and just kind of independently studied my way through. I did work with Chris and Jim. Chris worked it out so I could shoot on the animation stand there and Jim gave me a Bolex camera and a little copy stand that I still use. There was a lot of kindness there.

It was in Chicago that Mack created one of her first films, *A Joy* (2004), a commissioned piece for the band, For Tet.

I made it with this stained glass contact paper that was on the window of this apartment I was living in and the landlord wanted to take it off. So I was chiseling it off and was like, "Oh this is so cool" and "let's save this old, gooey crap for years, deteriorating in a bag and you know, glue it to film." That was all really exciting, but then it became "Woah, what do you do with this?" and it's all of the sudden a photographic medium as opposed to a painterly something.

Even though she was making cameraless films, Mack had an inherent interest in found materials that went back to high school.

For one project, I needed to make all these palm trees on a big backdrop piece of paper and I happened to find all these old telephone books. I started ripping out the pages to use as material to make the trees. Collage was definitely a place I went as soon as I started using the camera. I was really excited by people like Lewis Klahr, Martha Colburn and Stan Vanderbeek and seeing a lot of crude animation.

Mack also found camera-less filmmaking a bit restrictive.

I felt really bound early on by the limits of what we knew as abstraction. I was experiencing a kind of roadblock with camera-less filmmaking. It was cool, fun, and exciting, but what is actually possible here? "I think one of the things that was central to my actual experiments with camera-less filmmaking were the materials themselves, using colour pieces of plastic and often trying to scavenge those materials.

Much of the materials Mack uses in her films are from her own hoarding tendencies. "I think it started with, like, trash, and then I moved to domestic decorative objects which kind of evolved to, like, decorative objects in general." When she moved from Chicago to start teaching at Dartmouth, she realized she had a lot of fabric. "I took inventory of all my stuff under the camera to see if I could make a film. Once I saw that there was something there, I tried out different things."

All of Mack's films start with *stuff*. *New Fancy Foils* (2013) emerged from a package she received from animator George Griffin. "One day this beautiful book of foil samples showed up and he was like, 'I think these will come in handy one day.'" A couple of years later, Mack went back into the book and turned out a film. After exhausting the fabric road, Mack turned to other unusual materials like dollar store gift bags.

The gift bags were in a phase where I was moving to 3D. I started shooting all of this 3D stuff and made a film for special 3D glasses and did some live action. That was a moment where I was really interested in light, how it plays out in these different things.

Of late, Mack's interest has turned to plants and computer chips. "I'm on a utilitarian kick. Things, like computer chips, that are useful, but not necessarily beautiful or decorative."

This willingness and desire to tinker with almost anything tangible is what makes Mack's work so unique and refreshing. She eschews the standard paper-based cut-and-paste form (e.g. using old photos, magazine clippings etc.) in favour of an assortment of unconventional materials and even a somewhat different approach to the notion of collage.

At some point, I moved from a collage that's within a frame to a collage that's like a relationship, a temporal relationship with the film itself. You know I kind of went further out, back to Robert Breer and Scott Stark, who does a lot with flicker. He made this film with actually medical images of vaginas, and trees, and stuff. Again, using flicker, and of course with afterimage all these things take on these impressions. I'm really fascinated by this idea of a composite image that is only perceived. It's not really there, it's kind of a time collage.

Though technological advances have made collage (like all of animation) less time consuming, Mack says she's sort of shunned digital technology to a small degree.

I've partially ignored it in some ways as far as the direct capture and projection of my films is for the most part on 16mm. I definitely feel like the Bolex is my instrument and I love working with it. I love not being able to see what I'm doing for 4,000 frames at least.

That hasn't stopped Mack from embracing some aspects of digital technology. "I started in the 2000s. Video has always been a part of the equation; with every film, there's a video, there's many sound files, video edit, effects."

Mack's work has also addressed our iffy relationship with technology. *Glitch Envy (2010)* is a playful parody of the changing notion of "junk mail" in a social media era.

It was a time when new media was taking over and that's where the funding was, in new media, and in many ways I saw the new techniques of new media: dealing with the data of a video or something like that as completely parallel to camera-less filmmaking. You know, like, camera-less video-making in some way. As my films moved on, I became interested in technology replicating what already exists. Like your razor-blade icon looking like the razor-blade that actually cuts film.

Sing-songs and pretty fabrics aside, there are socio-economic and political undertones throughout much of Mack's work. The rapid flash-clash of patterns and materials hints at the volatile nature of capitalism and consumer waste. We produce, purchase and toss without much thought about the consequences or real need, but also beyond that, Mack also finds some sort of beauty in a lot of leftovers. Her use of these found objects often leads to musings about cultural appropriation, technology, human labour, domestic economics, and well, the implications of consumer culture in general.

Jodie Mack's films are brimming with jubilance, yet tinged with a hint of sadness. While Mack's films resuscitate the discarded and abandoned items of a wasteful hyper-capitalist society, it is a joy that is short-lived. The materials will still end up tossed and forgotten on some garbage heap.

Some of my films are little eulogies for materials. I think one reason that I'm really interested in animation is, for one reason or another, I'm obsessed with the idea of death and wanting to make that impossible. And so this idea of resuscitating what's about to go in the trash can to reveal its energy, and to give it you know, a celebration.

Moving on With Ainslie Henderson

IF YOU WANT TO see me cry and scream, just send me an animation film that recreates a hand-made technique digitally. You know, the ones where, say, they try to make it look like it's all made using paper when in fact it's just a flimsy recreation done on a computer. It's lazy, fraudulent and pointless. Thankfully there are also some talented contemporary animators like Ainslie Henderson who aren't afraid of a little hard work.

For his marvelous music video for the James song, *Moving On*, Henderson fashions a stop motion work made entirely out of wool. The result is an utterly inventive and heart-breaking piece of symbolism that superbly reflects the song's theme of loss and the tenuous and fragile string of existence.

The idea to use wool was in Henderson's mind from the get-go.

> I was walking around Edinburgh trying to think about ways of picturing death, playing the song over and over. There are loads of wool shops in town, and I was walking past, looking into one of them, and saw a big spool

of wool as the lyric in my headphones sang "time, always unwinding." It was pretty much all there in that moment.

While the idea and production (it took approximately 8 weeks to produce), *Moving On* was the first work that Henderson self-produced and that created new challenges and stresses. He notes:

> The challenge was trying to stay calm enough to focus, animate and sensitively tell the story, while being under that much pressure, juggling practical things like booking equipment, paying people and organizing the whole process. I also have a great respect for the band, so in the back of my mind was this pressure to honour them, I think that brought extra stress.

For decades now, music videos have been the source of some of the most original and daring work in animation. Artists are often given so much creative license that the work takes on the qualities of a personal short film. This experience was true of *Moving On*. Once the band approved the idea, Henderson was left to his own devices. "I think I checked in once during the process," says Henderson, "with production stills to share what I was doing. Tim Booth (the singer/lyricist of the band) wasn't sure about the puppets being without eyes (as my previous work relies on them so much to communicate emotion). I'm grateful he trusted me."

Later, Booth called Henderson to say it had made him cry.

It made me cry too, but in a good way.

CHAPTER 32

Peeping Wong Ping

Wıтн тнеıк вкıснт, popish colours, VHS tape-like glitchiness, and deadpan narration, Wong Ping's films have an aura of playful innocence tossed with a dose of giggly absurdities (Ping's *Fables* films mercilessly poke fun at the preachiness of Aesop and the like). Dive a little deeper though and you'll uncover a disturbed, violent and disengaged world filled with corruption, fecklessness, alienation, selfishness, suppressed emotions and a whole lot of lunacy.

If the Hong Kong artists' films seem unlike anything else on the animation circuit, it might be connected to the influence of, not Walt Disney or Miyazaki or anyone else in animation, but stand-up comedy. And like a good comedian (say George Carlin, Bill Hicks, Doug Stanhope), Ping's work makes you laugh at the uncomfortable. The best comedians are also sharp social critics who expose societal shortcomings, inconsistencies and downright stupidities.

"I like dark humour and jokes," says Ping. "It's not intentional, just my character." After one show, a critic was upset because he couldn't understand why the audience was laughing at horrible

DOI: 10.1201/9781003265153-32

moments in Ping's film. "This is when I realized that I use animation because no one really takes it seriously. My work is always about honesty and I think animation relaxes me. It's easier when no one takes you seriously." And certainly there's evidence of this everywhere. Some of the most caustic and uncomfortable scenarios in *Family Guy* or South Park, as obvious examples, would never have been permitted in a live-action setting. They get away with their parodies and alleged offensiveness because people, in their wisdom, don't take animation all that seriously. Comedy is in a similar boat. One of Richard Pryor's most memorable routines was about the time he set himself on fire while trying to freebase cocaine and rum (or something to that effect). Pryor was seriously injured at the time yet even he found humour in the absurdity of the situation. A day after being diagnosed with breast cancer, comedian Tig Notaro went on stage and performed a set about the experience. What else can one do in the darkest moments? Well, sure you can cry, but that's no fun. You can pray, but that's rather pointless. Why not laugh? When I had cancer, I cried behind the scenes, but mostly I laughed (granted, it was ball cancer so how someone with the emotional nature of a 15-year-old, not giggle at the prospect of losing a testicle?). Some might deem humour in such tragic moments as a means of distraction or avoidance, but I see it more as a form of acceptance, of accepting the ephemerality of existence.

And like the great comedians, Ping's films shock for the sake of it. Many of his films are rooted in a place of unharnessed honesty: *Who's the Daddy (2017)* was inspired by the time Ping's ex-girlfriend bitterly pranked him about being pregnant; *Stop Peeping (2014)* recounts a time when Ping spied on a neighbor. *Modern Way to Shower (2019)*, hilariously deals with Hong Kong protests, S&M culture and apathy in the face of peer pressure (Ping's joke about leaving a suicide note in a self-help book is pure gold), *Jungle of Desire* (2015) touches upon all sorts of issues from impotence and voyeurism to prostitution and corrupt cops.

"I like stuff that's surreal," adds Ping.

But that could be in our neighbourhood. So it's real and surreal. The base is solid, but the story can go wild. I like that tension. Half my stories come from my life and the rest come from the news and other places. Everything starts with my own experience.

Preparing for a show at the Guggenheim (yes, he's part of the fancy art world, but we'll revisit that later), Ping was riding around on bike with no ideas for the show.

Then I said this old man dragging a huge bag of mystery stuff that he threw in a bin. After he left I went over and pulled out the bag. It was filled with a huge amount of vhs porn tapes. I thought, "why is he throwing this out now, not when dvds took over or when PornHub took over?"

Ping immediately biked home and started writing a story about an elderly man that became *Dear, can I give you a hand* (2018), a sort of comic/tragic take on aging and conflicts between generations.

So, the Guggenheim. You see Wong Ping is a name on the contemporary art scene. For the last 10 years or so he's had one foot in the gallery scene (he's currently represented by two Galleries) and another in the animation world. Not bad for a guy who doesn't really like animation and rarely watched it as a kid. So, how did he get here?

Animation came slowly and reluctantly. In the early 2000s, Ping headed to Australia to take a multimedia design course at Curtin University.

I picked it because there were no exams or tests, only assignments. They try to teach you a little bit of everything like Photoshop, After Effects, film, drawings, production design. When I graduated in 2005 and returned to Hong Kong, I couldn't find a job. Hong Kong is very practical and you need to know the software to get into the animation industry. I couldn't find a job for six months and my parents were quite angry.

To make peace, Ping headed to the local library, signed out a book about After Effects and devoured it. "I made some really crappy drama and retouched scenes. Then I sent it to a broadcast station and they hired me. I suspect they needed cheap labour more than any skills I might have."

The job was not a pleasant experience for Ping. "It was very depressing. It's like we worked overtime in a cage almost every day. Imagine that everyday you're adjusting an actor's face, making a book or butt bigger." In need of a hobby to distract him from his daily workplace horrors, Ping had been writing. "They weren't short stories. I don't know what they were, but I felt very calm when writing."

Animation, or something like it, soon followed:

> One day I used this software at work to make something move. Back then it was this new thing called motion graphics. I don't even know if it's animation but it was easier for someone with no animation background. I thought it was cool and many music videos and shorts were being made using it instead of traditional animation. It was just so easy for me to manage because I have no skills. And I needed a hobby so it was perfect.

Meantime, Ping's stay at the broadcast studio ended after a couple of years. He ended up finding a job at Cartoon Network in Hong Kong. "It was quite interesting there.," says Ping. "At 10am they'd give you a brief and by 5pm you're supposed to finish a 10-second piece. So each day you had a new job. After a few years they moved to Singapore." Ping was also doing some illustration on the side for the news in Hong Kong and after work hours, he started to make his own shorts (e.g. *Peeping Tom*) that he would post online for anyone to see. Some of those who saw Ping's work were members of various Hong Kong indie bands. Three bands ended up approaching Ping to make music videos for them. The third video, *Under the Lion Crotch* (2013), won an award and cash prize. The win changed the course of Ping's life. Using the cash money, he immediately rented a studio space. "I paid for two years of rent with the prize money. During those two years I had no job or income but I created some of my first shorts and that's where it started getting attention from the art scene." Soon, Ping was invited to do a show (*Jungle of Desire*) by an indie Hong Kong art space. One of the attendees was Edouard Malingue who owned a noted gallery in Hong Kong. He loved the show and has been representing Ping ever since.

In terms of creative process, writing is the trigger for every film.

I spend more time writing and thinking about a story. When I write I don't think about the animation or how it would look. I just write. When it's almost done then I pass onto the character design and animation, but before that it's like luxury holiday because I can listen to stuff, watch stuff while I work . . . but when I write I can't do anything else. So I really enjoy the animation part. When I do it, I try not to think much about the story. I try to skip the link between the two. It's not like I designed a character for this story. If there's a depressed story, I don't want to draw a something to represent that depression. People can put it together at the end. It's more interesting for me this way.

Ping often approaches each film in a way that resembles a stand-up comedian. "I make hundreds of thoughts or fragments then I combine them to see if a story forms. Then I always try to improvise. I look for accidents when I'm animating. I find the animation process very mechanical, long and boring, but it gives me time to think and improvise."

Beyond process, some of the common features of Wong Ping's work are deadpan narration (often a lot of it), vibrant, eye-catching colours and a general avoidance (and this is music to my ears) of music. The toneless narration style came about simply because Ping couldn't find anyone do to voice-over.

> I care more about the text and I know how I want my written lines to be spoken so I decided to read them without tones. It's cheap and easy for me to do it but I think it works for me because I know the pacing I want. I think my voice is only background noise really. It works fine in an exhibition space where people can watch it again or online, but I think it can be tricky in a festival setting because it's often too fast.

The vibrant colour schemes were birthed in university.

> I took this course where they teach you about colour combinations in advertising. Like red on black is easier for people to read etc. . . . After one class I thought this was all bullshit. The colour wheel is for everyone. I mean I understand that this was for advertising or design, but I didn't enjoy the limitations. Then years later I discovered Illustrator and could pick any colour I wanted. There were no rules. I just pick mostly colours that hurt the eyeballs.

Given the brash in-your-face use of colour and dialogue, it seems somehow perfectly logical that Ping's films are relatively quiet.

> I use ambient noise, but I don't have time to make music. I enjoy using sound effects but I am not a fan of using music to bring emotion to people. I find it comforting to just use a couple of ambient sounds. I also never know when to stop talking and when I'd use music to break it up so I just avoid using it!

Ping's films also frequently reference a Hong Kong society in a flux. As natives try to silence the echoes of past British colonialism, while facing the usual daily economic and social struggles, along with the dark cloud of mainland China continuing to trickle into the Hong Kong atmosphere. The mainland China threat is particularly disconcerting. Ping admits that he is worried about Hong Kong's future. "A lot of friends are leaving. I don't see a better future in Hong Kong as China takes more control. People are scared and I think if this continues I would have to leave."

Through all of his varied work, whether for galleries or animation audiences, Ping uses provocative imagery and raunchy narratives to uncover deeper psychological and societal issues of desire, shame, obsession and alienation. By telling these stories with deadpan humour, animation and unflinching honesty, Ping humanizes difficult subject matters while asking us to consider why these are taboos in the first place.

CHAPTER 33

On the Weave of Construction

RISD Animation

THE RHODE ISLAND SCHOOL OF DESIGN's (RISD) track record in animation is pretty damn impressive for its success, longevity and range. RISD animation (which began in the late 1970s) gave us the creators of *Superjail* (Christy Karacas), *The Last Airbender* (Michael Dante Dimartino and RISD illustration major, Bryan Konietzko) and some animated series called *Family Guy* (Seth MacFarlane). There's also well-known media artists like Takeshi Murata and Ara Peterson along with an array of acclaimed indie artists like Fran Krause, Caleb Wood, Jesse Schmal, Leah Shore, Michael Langan, Max Porter, Emily Pelstring, Pilar Newton, Julie Zammarchi, Candy Kugel, Willy Hartland, the late Karen Aqua and many others familiar to the animation festival circuit. One graduate even went on to become an artisanal cheese maker.

Led by the initial teachings of Yvonne Anderson and later, Amy Kravitz, RISD animation films are consistently thoughtful,

DOI: 10.1201/9781003265153-33

eclectic and technically adventurous. The program has gone on to be recognized with numerous awards and critical acclaim. Over time, as the program grew, elective courses were added covering specialty areas of the field. Students can study character animation, character design, 3D CGI, Digital Compositing, Lighting, Directing, Sound for the Screen and more. RISD also has a well-developed puppet program.

With RISD films, you know you're going to get something different; work that takes risks, eschewing temporary trends and mainstream whims. Emphasizing concept over technique, there is a lo-fi feel to many of the films. The films are intimate, flawed, explorative and routinely engaging. Even the missteps are frequently more interesting than some of the best films from other animation schools. While it's misleading to lump RISD films into easy bake categories, there does tend to often be a split between dark or absurdist comedies and freewheeling experimentation.

Experimentation has long been a tradition at RISD, but the road towards a more absurdist-tinged tone arguably started in the late 1990s (at least that's about the time of my first memories of RISD films). Films like *Space War* (Christy Karacas, 1997), *Mr. Smile* (Fran Krause, 1999), *Sub* (Jesse Schmal, 2000), *Atlas Gets a Drink* (Mike Overbeck, 1999), *Brisket* (Joel Frenzer) and *Red Things* (Max Porter, 2003) were well received at festivals and clearly influenced future RISD students like Ryan Ines (*Violet*, 2015), *Talking Cure* (Felipe di Poi, 2016), *Toto's Tusks* (Mehr Chatterjee), *The Great Divide* (Brent Sievers), Masashi Yamamoto's films and of course, arguably the greatest tragic comedy of them all, *Lesley The Pony* (Christian Larave, 2014).

While the earlier films were seemingly broader, the later films serve up a darker psychological comedy. You can't help but feel a strong breeze of sadness blowing nearby, even while you're laughing at *Violet* (about a series of misfortunes upending an individual's life) and *Lesley (about sexual assault)* and even elements of Yamamoto's work (*Our Future, When You Touch Me*).

Comedy aside, RISD has consistently created some imaginative work that leans more towards the non-linear narrative or abstract side. *On The Weave of Construction* (Greg Buyalos, 1993) *Made in the Shade* (Takeshi Murata), *Edgeways* (Sandra Gibson), *12 Ball* (Ara Peterson), *Little Wild* (Caleb Wood), *Ripple* (Conor Griffith), *Toro* (Lynn Kim), *Doxology* (Michael Langan) and more recently, *Endless Forms Most Beautiful* (Meredith Binnette) all demonstrate the long-standing willingness to encourage students to take risks with their work, which lets them explore and stumble as they experiment with concepts and techniques. It's a logical approach that too few schools seem brave enough to embrace. For many, this might be their only opportunity to create their own work unhindered by outside pressures. It ain't cheap, so why not let out what is within you, rather than wasting time trying to impress someone else?

Of course, RISD animation is much more than these two streams. There have been broad based comedy (*Life of Larry*, Seth McFarlane) and more diversity-driven storytelling (e.g. *Mimi*, *Lotus Lantern*, *New Everyday*).

Overall, what separates RISD films from many animation schools is a burgeoning sense of playfulness and curiosity that thrives throughout the films, an almost naive willingness to explore and experiment with styles, tones, techniques. Let's just go in there, muck around and see what happens. This is not undertaken without purpose. You never feel that RISD students are necessarily rolling the dice or using techniques and tones just for the hell of it. Within each film you sense a unique and genuine identity within. In some cases, it's an attempt to locate that identity or voice and let it out, to let the world know . . . hey, this is me (or some fragment of me), warts and all.

—

The RISD Animation program is part of the Film/Animation/Video Department (FAV), which is under the Division of Fine Arts. The first animation equipment was purchased in 1971 and the first films were made by groups of students from other departments.

"When I was at RISD there was absolutely no one, no interest in animation," recalls

Candy Kugel, one of the earliest RISD students with an eye towards animation:

> During my first semester there, I saw there was someone giving a lecture up the hill at Brown University about his animation studio. I attended the talk and screening and had an epiphany that that was what I wanted to do.

The head of the Design and Illustration Department, Tom Sgouros, was Kugel's advisor:

> He agreed that I could do an animation independent study the following year. He then convinced the head of the film department, Ronald Banks, to allow me space in the film building (the Auditorium, where I commandeered the janitor's closet) and order the necessary animation supplies. And I was allowed use of the title camera when the film students weren't using it (but with no instruction)!

The following year (Kugel had left for Italy), RISD hired an animation teacher. After a year, that instructor departed and Yvonne Anderson took over. It was a decision that would have a lasting impact on RISD animation.

Anderson had already been running animation workshops for children (Yellow Ball Workshop) since the 1960s. The workshop had grown to the point where Anderson and assistants were giving animation workshops in Public schools. In the mid-1970s, Anderson was giving a presentation at the Art Director's club in Providence. She was then invited to do a talk and screening at RISD for the film and video students.

In 1977, Anderson received a call from FAV (Film, Animation, Video department) instructor Peter O'Neill:

> He said there was a vacancy in the animation program at RISD for the next year. Would I be interested in applying for the job? I asked him how much it paid. He mentioned the price, and I told him I would be home in a week, and would come over to discuss the situation.

Anderson ended up teaching two animation classes a week for beginners for five years before gradually increasing to 6 or 7 classes a year.

New York animator and artist, Willy Hartland (*The Viscera*, 1984), recalls the limited options for animators in those early days:

> In 1981, RISD students who wanted to study animation had two options: either major in illustration or in film/video and take animation courses," recalls animator, Willy Hartland (*The Visera*, 1984). "I opted to be an illustration major. However, film at RISD was very cool, 16mm and all about the Oxberry animation stands, the steenbeck, and the many Bolexes they had. (some of which were owned by Yvonne) There were only a few animation courses to take in those early days: Animation 1, which was 2 semesters, and focused on 2d animation techniques in the fall, and in the spring, 3d puppet animation and clay techniques were covered. Both courses were taught brilliantly by Yvonne Andersen.

Anderson's teaching had a profound impact on many students including award-winning animator, director and RISD teacher, Julie Zammarchi (*Portrait of Woman with Tomatoes*, 1982):

> Yvonne's classes were completely hands on and engaging. Her motto was "It doesn't have to be a masterpiece;

it just has to be done." Everyone's head was down and all hands were busy. I worked as her assistant for a while and that's when I really learned. In her no nonsense, practical way she had all of us helping each other and working together on our student projects. The tiny studios on the 4th floor of the auditorium building were always buzzing with energy.

Willy Hartland was equally influenced by both Anderson and Kravitz's teachings:

I was very fortunate to be there in the early 1980's, and to study with Yvonne and Amy. They had vastly different approaches to teaching animation. Yvonne focused more on the craft and technique, while Amy's pedagogy was very spiritual and metaphysical and all about guiding her students on a path toward finding their inner vision as artists. Animation in her view was not for entertainment but for personal expression. "If you're making people laugh," she would say "then you are not making a film for yourself, you are making a film for an audience." She also instilled in us something very important. She would make us realize that the animated film you are making now, is the most important thing in your life, because long after you are gone, your film will live on, and will be your legacy. To this day, I can't make a film any other way.

Anderson was without doubt the primary architect of the direction of the RISD animation program. As Amy Kravitz, Steve Subotnick and Agnieska Woznicka wrote in a 2016 article about RISD animation for the Melbourne Animation Festival,

Adept at finding simple solutions to complex problems, she believed in academic decisions by democratic rule, and she always did whatever needed to be done—whether that was cleaning up trash, repairing a camera, or writing reports. She was able to harness the creative and divergent energies of the FAV faculty into a powerful department.

It was around this time that another figure who would become an integral figure in RISD animation history. Amy Kravitz had started making films at age 11.

> I was in a summer program in Newton, MA. Yvonne was teaching that program. I loved it so much I started classes at Yellow Ball Workshop (which was actually Yvonne's home in Lexington, MA). I started assisting in classes when I was 14 at both places.

After graduating from Harvard in Social Anthropology, Kravitz became a teaching assistant for Dennis Pies in Harvard's animation program. In 1980 (or thereabouts, memories are foggy), she received an invitation from Yvonne Anderson to teach her own class at RISD:

> Yvonne had begun the program and the interested students needed a way to continue—there were only a few (about 5 students). The program grew and one advanced class grew to another advanced class and a "degree project" class. I had been exposed to a lot of new ideas from working with Dennis Pies—Yvonne and RISD gave me a lot of freedom to develop curriculum. Yvonne encouraged me to diverge from what she did in the introductory classes.

In 1984, Kravitz took a two-year hiatus from RISD to get her MFA at CalArts. She returned to RISD in 1986 armed

with more ideas and experiences. The courses I teach now have been in development since that time—I am constantly refining them. I still give some assignments that were the first ones I developed but I also add new ideas each year and my understanding continues to develop.

The third addition to the holy animation trinity at RISD arrived in the late 1980s. Steve Subotnick met (and later married) Kravitz while studying at CalArts. Later he started teaching part time at RISD. "I started as an administrator running their computers," says Subotnick. "Then I started teaching part time at RISD and the museum school in Boston. I think we had 8 students graduating then."

Subotnick was soon taking on more courses at RISD as the department continued to grow. Kravitz became full time in 1991. "Animation was the backbone of the department," adds Subotnick.

There was a big jump in the 1990s when studios started making features. It grew gradually from the late 80s to early 90s. We went from about 16 grads a year and then it jumped to 24 and pretty much stayed there.

For years, it was the trio of Anderson (until her retirement in 2003/04), Kravitz and Subotnick overseeing RISD animation.

Where RISD animation differs from other animation schools is through the encouragement of multidisciplinary study and the mandatory freshman foundation year. "No matter what you're studying, everyone starts off with the freshman foundation year. All doing the same drawing and design courses," says Subotnick. "You don't enter a department until the second year. You're obligated to take whoever wants to come into the department. The students choose."

Once in the animation program, students are then required to study live action filmmaking, video making and animation. "When students explore animation they have a deep artistic vocabulary with which to work—their thinking is not insular," says Kravitz.

Animation itself is a relatively small set of courses, however students bring inventive, energetic thinking, and rich skill sets to it thereby achieving excellent results. The classroom is an active laboratory and failure is seen as a necessary element of a successful journey.

The student voice is central to the program's success. "We try to have as little influence as possible," adds Subotnick. "We do try to encourage experimentation and the idea that each one of them has a unique voice." Subotnick believes the freshman foundation is a key part of this process.

It's a really rigorous program, an art boot camp. It really stretches their minds and makes them think about what they can do in new ways. They arrive with an idea about themselves and by the end of the first year they've given that up and opened their mind to all sorts of possibilities.

Now, while there's no arguing that Anderson, Kravitz and Subotnick have had a huge influence on the quality of films emerging from RISD, there have been other important voices through the years. "Brian Papciak is a passionate filmmaker who really pushed us to use our 'voice' in our work and make creative decisions with great intentionality (even if that intention was difficult to verbalize—as long as it made sense in the context of the film)," says Michael Langan (*Doxology*, 2007). "Dan Sousa and Jeff Sias were also gifted working animators who supported that culture of thoughtfulness and innovation."

"Bryan Papciak is also a huge influence on the quality of work coming out of the school," adds Oscar nominee and current RISD instructor, Max Porter.

I remember that Bryan screened *The Passion of Joan of Arc* [dir. Carl Dreyer] and brilliantly deconstructed how this complex narrative was built off of a sequence of simple close-ups. He hammered home that even if animation has its own language, it's still part of a larger cinematic vocabulary. He pushed us to dig deeper and challenged our assumptions about what we were doing.

Another element of RISD's success is the exposure of all types of international animation to the students. This is done via annual visits to the Ottawa International Animation Festival, guest talks and an impressive collection of films accessible to all students. "Amy has a collection of the best animation films in history, open for viewing," says Caleb Wood (*Little Wild*, 2010).

When I was there, I felt like I was exposed to everything that really matters in the animation world. I believe Amy has figured out the right moments in each student's development in which they are ready to see a certain film from the shelf. She waits to see a spark in your work that correlates to one of the films on her shelf. Then she shows you, and you become a little bit more enlightened.

While a (very) few have expressed concerns about RISD's lack of industry training, most welcomed it. "RISD was great for keeping me sheltered from the professional world," says Fran Krause, who now teaches animation at CalArts.

I can't really recall any guest lecturers that were professional working studio animators. We were able to develop our styles and films without really worrying about getting jobs. This was very helpful, as I see a lot of students only working on animation in order to get a job in the industry, and that's a very depressing and unfulfilling way to approach animation.

Noah Gallagher (*Papa Sun*, 2020), crossed the U.S. to attend RISD. "My high school art teacher, Carlotta Maggi, introduced me to RISD," says Gallagher. It was a leap of faith that took me from California to Rhode Island to study art. I then picked the animation department, based on my interest and curiosity of moving drawings." Before that, Gallagher tried animation in high school but found it overwhelming and discouraging. The experience at RISD was the polar opposite:

> RISD's animation department really gave me a space to make "bad art." Once I stopped taking myself and the medium so seriously, I started to really fall in love with animation. I was able to try a plethora of creative mediums while being surrounded by incredibly creative minds. I was learning from my peers just as much as I was from my professors. The professors took time to individually understand and know each student. They wanted us to bring our visions to life, and they provided the necessary tools and resources to do so.

I could go on and on about RISD's history and successes, but we have to stop somewhere, so why not end with a darkly comic, yet utterly loving quote from animator and RISD grad, Jesse Schmal (*Sub*, 2000) that fittingly matches the absurdist tone of a number of RISD animation films:

> Yoda gets thrown around often as a descriptor for their instructional style, and disagree I would not. Someday, I plan to off either Amy or Steve—whomever puts up less of a fight—to be faculty there; I would miss Amy or Steve of course, but carrying on the RISD way of independence and vision would be a noble workday.

CHAPTER 34

Lesley the Pony
Has an A+ Day

INCREDIBLY, A LARGE CHUNK OF people still seems to believe that an animation film necessitates an experience that will be light and funny. And sure, Pixar, Disney and so-called "adult" animation (a vile term that should be eradicated from language) like *The Simpsons* and *Family Guy* have not done much to counter that skewed vision.

Even on the animation festival circuit—where folks are supposed to be more sensitive and sophisticated (ha! Now THAT's funny!), I routinely hear mild moans and groans about the dearth of "funny" animation films—often these come from people well versed in the diversity of independent animation.

My response is two-fold, one: please point me to the legal document that mandates animation must by nature be funny and two: most of the so-called "serious" films frequently possess a good dose of dark humour. If you can't recognize that, then maybe re-think your definition of humour.

That said . . . I'd love to show more comic films. I have minimal patience for intelligent, earnest but utterly humourless films (see The Brothers Quay, Simon Pummell). We go through this ride once and if you can't find a way to try your best to laugh through most of it, well . . . you're fucked.

In general, animators actually don't make funny films. Yes, *they* think (as do their classmates, teachers and parents) their film is a gut-buster of comic gold, but in truth it's usually little more than a faded Xerox of a rejected scene from a generic studio production they adored as a teenager.

I like my comedy with a dose of bitterness, a dash of absurdity along with a speckle of truth—and that's hard to come by—whatever the medium.

Which leads me to *Lesley The Pony Has an A+ Day (made, according to the credits, by a 4th grader named Wesley Nunēz)*, a wonderfully dark and demented piece of silliness that nails the often hilarious, surreal and hyper-violent world of children's drawings/creations.

Upon first viewing, it's easy to swim in the innocence of Lesley's song and joyful gallop and emerge soaked from a flood of tearful laughter, but look a little closer and you suddenly see a ghastly horror film about a troubled—and possibly abused—4th grader.

It all starts out so innocently. Lesley is en route to Merryville to see the Duke. The journey is filled with blissful thoughts of anticipation and wonder (and elves and tulips). This all starts to go haywire once Lesley and the Duke meet and talk turns from the pony's tardiness to an awkward talk of the Duke's troubled love life.

That's when things start to unravel for our young Pony as he gallops on while "dying on the inside" and "emotionally void" before unleashing an unharnessed stream of violence. The screen explodes into a cacophony of chaos and blood-like imagery. When Lesley finally simmers, there are no more elves or tulips. Blood slowly seeps beneath the door that once housed the happy monkeys. A fire burns in Merryville.

I'm scared. Is this about Lesley a pony or Wesley a 4th grader? Is the Duke a stand-in for Wesley's teacher, Mr. Matuk?

Forget what I said . . . it's too much . . . too dark . . .

Please just sing the song . . . just sing the song . . . make the bad thoughts go away . . .

"Lesley . . . prancing through the streets of Merryville . . ."

There, there . . . everything will be okay.

Right?

*Lesley was in fact made by Christian Larrave as his graduate film at the Rhode Island School of Design—the very same school *Family Guy* creator Seth MacFarlane attended as an animation student.

Index

Note: Page numbers in **bold** indicate tables, and those in *italics* indicate figures

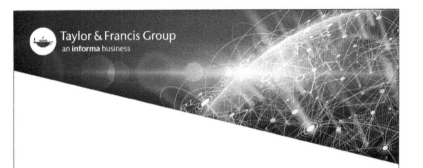